THE
WINE LOVER'S
—GUIDE TO—
Champagne
and North-East France

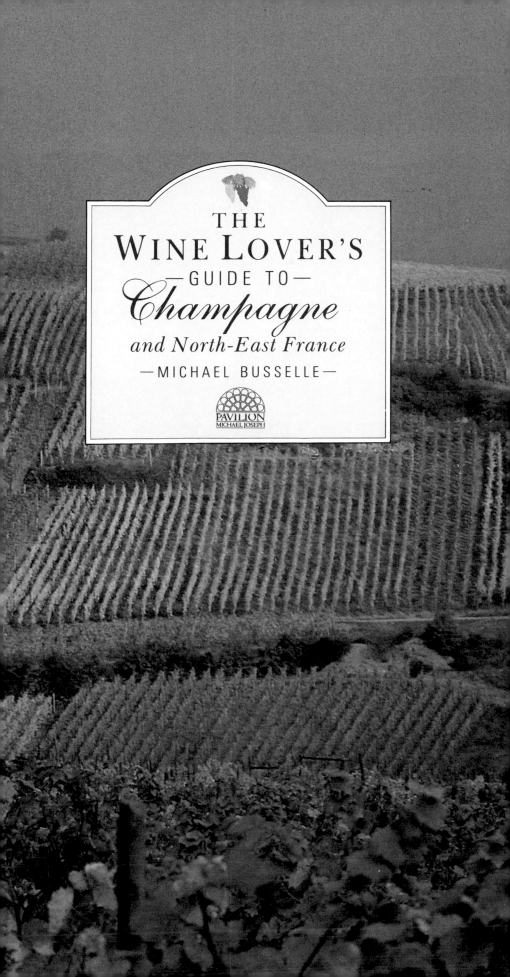

THE
WINE LOVER'S
—GUIDE TO—
Champagne
and North-East France
—MICHAEL BUSSELLE—

PAVILION
MICHAEL JOSEPH

First Published in Great Britain in 1989 by
PAVILION BOOKS LIMITED
196 Shaftesbury Avenue, London WC2H 8JL
in association with Michael Joseph Limited
27 Wrights Lane, Kensington, W8 5TZ

Photographs and wine tours text
copyright © Michael Busselle 1986
Wine-buying guides compiled by Graham Chidgey &
Lorne Mackillop copyright © Pavilion Books 1986
Other text by Ned Halley copyright © Pavilion Books 1989

Series Editor Ned Halley
Designed by Bridgewater Design Ltd
Maps by Lorraine Harrison

A CIP catalogue record for this book is available from the
British Library

ISBN 1-85145-244-3

10 9 8 7 6 5 4 3 2 1

Printed and bound in Spain by Cayfosa Industria Grafica

Contents

Introduction

Vineyards above the village of Villers-Marmery

OURING THE VINEYARDS AND WINERIES of Champagne, Alsace and the Jura offers introductions to some of the most distinctive of all French wines. At the famous *maisons* of Champagne – the likes of Moët, Mumm and Taittinger – visitors discover the secrets of *vin mousseux*. In the impossibly picturesque properties of the Alsace winemakers you will taste some of the best white wines in the world. And in the Jura, rustic *vignerons* proudly show off new wines that will last for a hundred years.

Seen in the making and tasted in the ambiance of its own region, every wine takes on an extra dimension. To learn a little about the land, and the grapes, and the method of production, can suddenly make sense of the jumble of information most of us have accumulated about wine, but have never really been able to relate to actual tastes.

All the wines suggested among the 'Cases for Tasting' are exported. So if you are strictly an armchair tourer, you need travel no further than your local merchant to find quite a number of them. Buying wine *in situ*, of course, is more fun – but there are a few points that it is wise to follow.

VENTE DÉGUSTATION

A notable advantage of shopping at the farm gate is that you can taste before you buy. Some growers, particularly the smaller ones, display *Vente Dégustation* or *Caveaux de Dégustation* ('tasting and sales' or 'taste in our cellars') signs at the roadside. Bigger establishments may well have their own shop, selling a wide range of their products. Many co-operatives sell as much as half of all their wines direct to private customers.

Grapes loaded ready for the first pressing

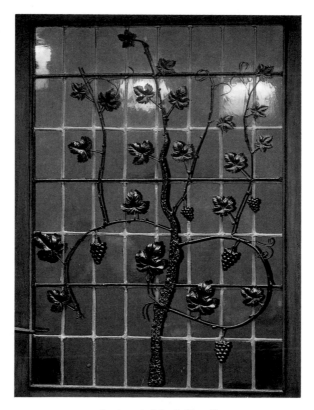

A restaurant window in Riquewihr

Autumnal vineyards near Damery

Not all *vignerons*, it must be said, offer *vente directe* to the public. Some sell all of their production to *négociants* (brokers). Others simply lack the facilities – or the will – to deal with the paperwork.

If you are particularly keen to buy the wine of a certain grower but are unsure of whether *vente directe* is offered, write in advance of your departure to France. The address should be on the bottle label (or at least enough of an address for your letter to reach its destination). Or you can look it up in one of the comprehensive guides such as *The Macdonald Guide to French Wines* (Macdonald Orbis).

PRICES

Winemakers in Champagne and Alsace – and to a lesser extent in the Jura – operate on a big scale throughout the world's market for fine wines. They are therefore understandably reluctant to undercut the myriad retailers who stock their wares worldwide. Therefore it is best not to expect bargain prices if you are buying direct from a winemaker with big overseas sales. (Some Champagne houses charge more in their own shops than you would pay in large-turnover retailers in Britain and the USA, especially when the value of the French franc is down.)

From smaller concerns such as the *récoltant-manipulants* in Champagne, who sell a very high proportion to private customers calling for a case or two to cram into the Citröen, you can expect a much better deal. First-rate champagnes at Jean Moutardier's Breuil vineyards in the Marne, for example, cost £5 to £6 – perhaps half what they might cost abroad.

A village house in Oger

Most *vignerons* selling direct will have a printed tariff card. Others chalk their prices up on a blackboard – with suitable elevations according to the season. Some post no prices at all and doubtless charge each customer what they like.

If you find prices unattractive, or the grower reluctant to sell any wine at all, ask whether he has an agent in your home country.

TRAVELLING WITH WINES

Assuming that you will be travelling by car, remember that wines do not like extremes of temperature. If bottles are left in the boot of a parked car in sunshine, the wines can seep past their corks as the temperature rises, and are thus completely ruined. Direct sunlight shining through the windows of estate cars onto wine has a similar devastating effect.

In winter, severe frost can freeze wines left out in a car overnight. The freezing liquid pushes the corks out, ruining the wine – and probably doing very little to beautify your upholstery.

Try always to keep the wines in conditions as similar as possible to the cellar from which they came; this does make a good deal of difference to its drinkability, so it is well worth taking the trouble.

Finally, if it seems likely that you will buy more bottles than the customs regulations permit on a duty-free basis, do remember to ask for receipts for all the wines concerned. You will be asked to pay duty and tax on all the bottles by which you exceed the limit. (An important consideration when calculating whether local purchases are really good value.)

FOOD

As for all the wonderful foods that proliferate in every region of France – with Champagne, Alsace and the Jura proving no exception to the rule – the choice is vast. Gastronomic specialities such as Champagne's *andouillettes de mouton*, the *foie gras* of Strasbourg in Alsace (said to be the finest in the world), or the exotic *morilles* fungi from the Jura are all-but impossible to find outside France. And in those few city delicatessens that do import such rare delights, you can count on prices very much higher than at source.

All the hotels and restaurants mentioned from page 88 offer regional specialities on their menus as well as, naturally, vast selections of the local wines. Prices for both vary according to the grandeur of the establishment, of course. As far as the cooking is concerned, there is obvious justification for the higher prices in the Michelin three-star restaurants than those prevailing in the humble *auberge* down the road.

Wines, on the other hand, are the same whether you dine out on the 25 FF *menu touristique* or the 600 FF *menu gastronomique*. Such is the enthusiasm for wine among French restaurateurs as a race that you can expect a wonderful choice at even the simplest of places – and a chance to try them at approachable prices. Conversely, in a very smart and expensive restaurant where the food is of a higher standard altogether, it makes sense to let the spectacular French *cuisine* occupy centre stage and stick to straightforward (not to say less ruinously expensive) wines that won't hog the limelight.

Where viticulture gives way to agriculture near Tours-sur-Marne

A Tour of Champagne

Pages 12–13: Entering Graves. Above: Vineyards near Venteuil

*T*HE CHAMPAGNE VINEYARDS, the most northerly in France, are less than two hours' drive from Paris and only slightly further from the ports of Calais and Boulogne. The city of Reims is the centre of the champagne industry, although Epernay closely rivals it and the nearby town of Ay is also important. Most of the major champagne houses have their headquarters in one of these three towns and each would make an ideal base from which to explore the vineyards. You must visit one of the champagne houses. They are built in the vast caverns and miles of tunnels, many dating back to Roman times, carved out of the chalky hills. Here millions of bottles of champagne are stored – an awe-inspiring sight. Most of the major houses actively welcome guests, often without formal appointments, and will take you on a guided tour showing you how the wine is made, and you can also taste and buy some champagne. The cellars of Pommery & Greno in Reims are particularly impressive: they have seventeen kilometres of tunnels and caverns cut into the chalk up to thirty metres below the surface.

THE WINES

Originally the wines of the Champagne region were still rather than sparkling. In the seventeenth century it was discovered that if – instead of being left to ferment completely in wooden casks – the wine was bottled at an early stage, the fermentation would continue inside the bottle and, since the air was trapped, the gas given off by the process would dissolve in the wine. The result was that when the pressure was released by removing the cork, the wine was found to be full of millions of tiny little bubbles.

Demand for this sparkling wine, particularly by the English, led to the perfection of the technique known as the 'Champagne method' (which is used to make some other wines too). The grapes are picked, pressed and begin their fermentation in casks in the usual way. But here the work of the *vigneron* stops and the shipper takes over. The wine is taken to one of the champagne towns – Reims, Epernay or Ay – to the shipper's *maison*. Here a small amount of sugar is added to stimulate the continuing fermentation, then it is bottled and stored in the enormous underground cellars cut into the chalk. To keep the wine clear of the sediment that would otherwise accumulate, the bottles are stored pointing head down in special racks (*pupitres*) so that the sediment drops towards the cork. Every day over a period of several months the bottles are given a little twist to encourage this (a procedure known as *remuage*). When all the sediment has settled the cork is removed, the small amount of

Above: The house of Castellane in Epernay.
Left: Veuve Clicquot's cellars in Reims

wine containing it is released (a process called *dégorgement*), the bottle is topped up with more of the same wine, and a new cork put in. The bottles need to be especially strong and the corks wired down to contain the pressure of the gas within.

The bubbles created by this natural process (as opposed to the artificially injected gas which makes soft drinks, and even some wine, fizzy) are small and gentle, spread evenly throughout the wine and last for a long time. *Crémant* is the term used for a wine with a gentler, more subdued sparkle.

During the re-fermentation in the bottle all the sugar in the wine is used up. The resulting very dry champagne is called *brut*. If sweeter champagnes are required a little sweetened wine is added at the *dégorgement* stage, in varying quantities: the results are dry (*extra sec* or *extra dry*); slightly sweet (*sec*); sweeter (*demi-sec*) or sweet (*doux*).

Vineyards near the village of Bouzy

Champagne is made from a blend of different sorts of grapes; the blend is called the *cuvée*. In the seventeenth century, the famous cellar master of the Abbey of Hautvillers, Dom Pierre Pérignon, was the first to perfect the technique of blending to improve the quality and balance of champagne. The balance of the wine is adjusted by both the selection of the grape types and by the combination of wine from different vineyards and, in some cases, from different years. (Vintage or *millésimé* is champagne made from the grapes of one year only). The grapes used are the white Chardonnay, grown in the Epernay region, the Pinot Noir (Montagne de Reims and Vallée de la Marne), and Pinot Meunier.

White champagne is produced from these last two black grapes by extracting the juice rapidly in shallow presses and removing the skins quickly to prevent them from giving their red colour to the wine (to make red wine the skins are left in for longer). Blanc de Blancs is white wine made exclusively from white grapes. Some rosé champagne is made by mixing a little red wine in with the white, a practice not permitted in other regions. The traditional way to make rosé is to allow the skins of the black grapes to colour and impart flavour to the juice, as in Mailly-Champagne.

There is also the usual distinction of *crus*, the wines from the best vineyards. Those with the most favourable siting and soil are designated *Grands Crus*. There are twelve of these: Ambonnay, Avize, Ay, Bouzy, Cramant, Louvois, Mailly, Puisieux, Sillery, Tours-sur-Marne, Verzenay and Beaumont-sur-Vesle; there are a further forty-eight communes, too many to list here, which qualify as *Premiers Crus*, a slightly lower quality.

Champagne, however, is not the only wine made in this region. Still red and white wines, and a little rosé, are produced under the appellation *Coteaux Champenois*. These wines are made from the same three grape types used for champagne, they are bottled in the same elegantly distinctive bottles and sealed with the same cork. The best known of these wines has a name that appeals to English wits – Bouzy Rouge. Ratafia is another regional wine. It is sweetish and fortified, rather similar to Pineau des Charentes, and is usually drunk chilled as an apéritif. Marc de Champagne is a fortified wine made with the *marc* (a distillation of the mud-like residue of grape skins, pips and stems left after pressing the grape juice for the champagne).

THE CUISINE

The cuisine of the Champagne region, although excellent, is not as distinctive as in some other areas of France. Champagne is featured in a variety of dishes. In *poulet au champagne*, for example, the chicken is simmered in champagne. Freshwater fish are often served in champagne-based sauces, such as *écrevisses au champagne* (freshwater crayfish poached in a *court-bouillon* containing champagne). A sorbet made from Marc de Champagne is often served as palate freshener between courses.

The great French cheese *Brie* comes from near here; a slice from a large flat, creamy *Brie de Meaux* is a revelation if you have only experienced the bland, plastic versions so often found in supermarkets; *Brie de Melun* and *Brie de Coulommiers* are two other types worth looking out for. *Maroilles* is a creamy

Preparing the grapes for the second pressing

Landscape and vineyards near Avize

cow's-milk cheese with a rust-coloured crust and a rich smell and flavour. The fruit is also excellent in this region. The *rousselet* pear of Reims is highly prized, as are the cherries from Dormans.

THE ROUTES DES VINS *Michelin Map 56*

There are three sections in the Champagne Route des Vins: the Montagne de Reims, which lies between Reims and Epernay; the Vallée de la Marne, and the Côte des Blancs, the most southerly vineyards of the region. There are additional areas of vineyards entitled to the Champagne appellation still further to the south in the valley of the Aube. I have suggested that you start the route from the direction of Reims but it would be a simple matter to join the circuit at any convenient point.

The only reason the Montagne de Reims is clearly visible from the city – 'mountain' is a slight exaggeraton since it is only a few hundred metres high – is because of the unrelieved flatness of the surrounding plain. There are vines on the slopes of the hill; on its northern side the vineyards and fields of corn and other crops extend on to the plain below.

Take the Château-Thierry road from the city, the RD 380; you will soon be climbing the

Harvesting the grapes near Verzenay

slope of the Montagne towards the wine village of Jouy-lès-Reims. The wine route turns to the east now, along the D 26. At the small wine village of Ville-Dommange, there is a lovely twelfth-century church, and the pretty hilltop chapel of St Lie hidden in a copse on the slopes above the vineyards; from the narrow lane which climbs up behind the village to the chapel you will get some beautiful sweeping views north and west.

The route continues through the village of Sacy, which has a fine Romanesque church, to Sermiers, on the main road between Epernay and Reims, the N 51. Cross this and continue along the D 26 to a succession of small villages close to the top of the Montagne: Rilly-la-Montagne, from where there are superb views of the plain below and distant Reims; Ludes, a tiny village virtually taken over by the establishment of Canard-Duchêne; and Mailly-Champagne, a *Grand Cru* commune famous for its rosé. Verzenay also has *Grand Cru* vineyards overlooked by its distinctive windmill, a feature that can be seen from far away.

The next stop is Verzy, and from here you can make a detour to Mont Sinai, the highest point of the Montagne, and also to the Faux de Verzy, an extraordinary forest of gnarled and misshapen trees that look like giant bonsais. The wine route continues around the side of the Montagne, now providing vast panoramas to the east with the fields of corn stretching away into the distance – in summertime, the lush green vineyards are in vivid contrast to the golden fields below. This was where I watched a helicopter pilot spraying the vines; with ease he made his craft duck and weave among them, often disappearing into a hollow below the tops of the vines.

Previous pages: Looking down towards the Marne. Above: The five Deutz champagnes.

As the wine route continues through the village of Trépail towards Ambonnay and Bouzy, it begins to descend from the Montagne. The village of Bouzy, famed for its still red Coteaux Champenois wine, marks the point where the vines give way to other crops. You begin turning westwards towards the valley of the Marne. Tours-sur-Marne is set beside the canal that runs parallel to the river and houses the headquarters of Laurent-Perrier. Mareuil-sur-Ay is also by the canal; you should walk up the narrow vineyard roads in the hill above the village and look out over the Marne Valley.

Ay is a much larger town and is the base of a number of important champagne houses, including Deutz & Geldermann, Ayala and Bollinger; it is one of the *Grand Cru* communes. There is a Musée Champenois here which displays ancient tools and implements used in vine cultivation and wine-making. From here a brief detour can be made through the Val d'Or to the villages of Avenay-Val-d'Or and Louvois, which has a twelfth-century church and a privately owned château. From Ay, the wine road joins the main N 51 on the outskirts of Epernay. However, drive back towards Reims up the winding hairpin bends to the village of Champillon, then to the Royal Champagne Hotel further up the hill at Bellevue; its rooms border the vineyards, and it has an excellent restaurant which serves a special Marc de Champagne sorbet.

Returning to Dizy along the main road you can continue westward along the Marne Valley taking the D 1 towards Château-Thierry; the road runs alongside the river for most of the journey. You must take a short detour to the village of Hautvillers, high up on the slopes. Dom Pérignon was cellar

Vineyards and wheatfields near Bergères-lès-Vertus

The Canal de la Marne seen from the vineyards above Mareuil-sur-Ay

*Right: Côtes des Blancs, the village
of Monthelon bathed in sunlight*

master to the Benedictine abbey here which is now owned by Moët &
Chandon. The road continues through a succession of wine villages such as
Cumières (a *Grand Cru* commune), Damery and Venteuil to Châtillon-sur-
Marne, where the vast, monolithic statue of its most famous son, Pope Urban
II, dominates the town from high on the hill above. At Verneuil the road
rejoins the main RD 380. You can return directly to Reims; alternatively,
continue to Dormans, where you can cross the river and start the route
through the Côte des Blancs.

Instead of taking the main road, the N 3, direct to Epernay, a quieter and
more interesting route follows the D 222 through the small wine villages of
Oeuilly, Boursault and Vauciennes towards St Martin-d'Ablois, Vinay and
Moussy. As the road climbs up out of the valley there are some fine views of
the Montagne on the other side of the river. Here the vines are almost

exclusively Chardonnay and the landscape is generally flatter, with gentle hills creating slight contours.

This part of the tour is quite short and meanders through a sequence of small villages, including Monthelon, Chavot, which has a hilltop church set among the vines, Courcourt, from where there are lovely views, Grauves, Cramant and Avize – the latter two are *Grand Cru* communes.

The southern limit of the tour is reached along the D 9 through the villages of le Mesnil-sur-Oger and Vertus to Bergères-lès-Vertus. Here there is quite a different atmosphere and character from the countryside nearer the Marne; the land is very flat, with only occasional hilly outcrops, and the sky appears to be endless. Climb to the top of Mont Aimé to the south of Bergères-les-Vertus; there is a Table d'Orientation here which is a perfect place to open a bottle of champagne and drink to the fruitful land below.

A Grande Marque Case For Tasting

OF MORE THAN TWO HUNDRED CHAMPAGNE HOUSES, dozens count themselves *Grandes Maisons*, claiming to produce superior wines. This selection of just some of those great names represents a cross-section of the many champagne styles now so widely enjoyed throughout the world.

BOLLINGER

The rich and distinctive wines of this *chic* firm are made largely from the black-skinned Pinot Noir grape. Bollinger RD – *récemment dégorgé* – has remained up to ten years in bottle with the yeasty detritus of fermentation before being disgorged. The result is a glorious intensity of flavour. 350FF.

HEIDSIECK

Heidsieck & Co. Monopole is among several *grandes marques* making a rosé wine by blending red and white champagne. Heidsieck rosé is a single-vintage champagne with a delicate pink colour, *brut* (very dry) in style but positively fruity in flavour. Good with food. 150FF.

LANSON

Black Label Brut is a zippy, almost lemony-tasting non-vintage alive with youthful freshness. In spite of the name, it is made about equally from black and white grapes. Founded in 1760, Lanson is now second in size only to Moët & Chandon. 100 FF.

LAURENT-PERRIER

Brut LP is this large firm's basic non-vintage champagne, crisply fresh, but distinctly fruity. 110FF. LP's lovely Cuvée Brut Rosé is made by the traditional – and now rare – technique of allowing the skins of Pinot Noir grapes to impart some of their colour into the wine during fermentation. 150FF.

LOUIS ROEDERER

Cristal, the great vintage wine of this distinguished house, is among the very best of all champagnes – some say *the* best. So known because it comes in a clear-glass bottle, it is consistently wonderful, even in poorer vintage years. Cristal is rich, 'toasty' and lingering in flavour with good body to balance its exciting freshness. 350FF.

MOËT & CHANDON

By far the largest champagne house, Moët (correctly pronounced Mo-ette) sells some twenty-four million bottles a year, most of it their non-vintage Brut Imperial, or Première Cuvée as it is labelled for Britain. The wine has a fine gold colour and fruity, appealing flavour. 100FF.

DOM PÉRIGNON

Moët's prestige wine takes its name from the Benedictine monk popularly – but erroneously – credited with 'inventing' champagne. Dom Pérignon deserves its fame, though, as the leading 'luxury' champagne, with its beautifully subtle *mousse* (froth) and complex depths of flavour – not to mention the memorably elegant bottle. 350FF.

GH MUMM

Cordon Rouge, labelled with its unmistakable red sash, has been Mumm's standard non-vintage wine since 1875. *Brut* in style, this champagne is nevertheless a little sweeter than most of its rivals; but it is fresh and lively and has special appeal for drinkers unaccustomed to the acidity of many champagnes. 110FF.

PERRIER-JOUET

The fresh-cut-flowers aroma and youthfully zesty flavour of their non-vintage *brut* wine are, PJ say, the product of the very high quality Chardonnay grapes, grown in their own top-rated vineyards at Cramant in the Côte des Blancs area, which make up a quarter of the *cuvée* (grape blend) for this superb champagne. 100FF.

POL ROGER

Extra Dry White Foil has borne a black border round its label in mourning tribute to Sir Winston Churchill, Pol Roger's most revered customer, since his death in 1965. Today, this non-vintage champagne remains very distinguished: a fine, pale-gold colour, creamy *mousse* and rich flavour. 100FF.

POMMERY

Brut Royal, the non-vintage wine, is among the lighter-bodied and more delicately flavoured of the *grande marque* champagnes, very fresh and with a vigorous *mousse*. 130FF. Pommery has the historic distinction of having launched the first *brut* champagne in 1874. Until then, all champagnes had been sweet.

VEUVE CLICQUOT

Yellow Label Brut is full-bodied and richly scented, deep and slightly sweet in flavour – absolutely delicious. Nicknamed 'The Widow' after Nicole Clicquot (*née* Ponsardin) who took over the business on her young husband's death in 1805 and made champagne famous worldwide, this wine sells five million bottles annually. 140FF.

A Further Case For Tasting

MANY OF THE CHAMPAGNE WINEMAKERS whose names are less familiar than those of the major *marques* nevertheless produce wonderful wines, both sparkling and still. The following twelve are among the most admired by enthusiasts who know that a big name is by no means everything.

ABEL LEPITRE

Cuvée 134 is a *blanc de blancs* champagne, made entirely from white Chardonnay grapes. This makes for a very crisp, fresh wine, but with an appealing 'toasty' aroma. It is one of six champagnes made by Lepitre, a firm only recently becoming known outside France. 100FF.

BRUNO PAILLARD

The youngest of all champagne houses, founded in 1981 by the enterprising M. Paillard, then only twenty-eight. His lively and elegant vintage wines each have labels designed by different artists 'to reflect the personality of the wine'. They are consistent, though, in their freshness and fullness of flavour. 150FF.

CANARD-DUCHÊNE

Owned by Veuve Clicquot and rather overshadowed by its famous parent, Canard-Duchêne nonetheless makes an exceptionally good non-vintage champagne. Its layers of delicate but deep flavour linger in the mouth, and make this a delicious – and well-priced – wine to enjoy with food. 90FF.

HENRIOT

Largely made with white Chardonnay grapes, the non-vintage champagne of this 1808-founded firm is described rather disarmingly by Henriot as 'a nervous, extra-dry wine, with complex aromas, which does not hesitate to assert its origin'. A fruity and well-flavoured champagne full of character. 110FF.

JACQUESSON

Signature is a 'luxury' champagne from this very distinguished firm, based in the charmingly named village of Dizy. With its fine *mousse* and sublime balance of fruitiness and fresh acidity, it rivals many better-known luxury wines – and is comparatively inexpensive. 140FF. Jacquesson also produce a beautiful Blanc de Blancs non-vintage. 90FF.

JEAN MOUTARDIER

Moutardier is a *récoltant-manipulant*, which means he makes his champagne entirely from grapes grown in his own vineyard – in this case a modest twenty-five acres in the Marne valley. Moutardier's non-vintage *brut* wine is fruitily scented with a fine, mature flavour which lingers in the mouth. Outstanding value. 60FF.

GEORGE GOULET

Under the same ownership as Abel Lepitre, George Goulet has an improving range of wines, including a firmly flavoured *brut* non-vintage made largely with Pinot Noir and Pinot Meunier black grapes. Good quality, fruity champagne with a pleasing gold colour. 100FF.

MERCIER

Owned by Moët, this is the brand the company reserves mainly for France, while most of the Moët wines are exported. Mercier Brut is a richly coloured and appealingly freshly flavoured champagne of real quality. The green-labelled Extra Rich Mercier is a sweet sparkler to drink with puddings. 70FF.

RUINART

The oldest champagne house, founded in 1729 by a nephew of Benedictine monk Dom Thierry Ruinart who was a contemporary of Dom Pérignon, Ruinart produces an excellent range at low prices. The *brut* non-vintage is a racy, almost lemony wine that is light in body and very fresh. 90FF.

COTEAUX CHAMPENOIS

This is the still wine that is, in effect, the ancestor of champagne, which only became a sparkling wine in the 1700s. Laurent-Perrier's Blanc de Blancs, made entirely with white Chardonnay grapes, is pale in colour, extremely dry and refreshingly sharp on the palate. An acquired taste. 50FF.

BOUZY ROUGE

Delightfully named – after the commune where the vineyards are – this is the best still red wine of Champagne. Most of it is used for blending in *rosé* champagne, but in its own right Bouzy can be an elegant and fruity wine in the burgundy style. It improves with age. Makers include Abel Lepitre and Jacquesson. 30–100FF.

ROSÉ DES RICEYS

The rare pink wine of the Aube. It is made from Pinot Noir grapes, vinified to allow their dark skin colour to impart a reddish-orange glow to the white wine. It has a very fine flavour reminiscent of cherries and peaches. Alexandre Bonnet's Rosé des Riceys is an excellent example. 70FF.

A Tour of the Aube

Left: A village house in Les Riceys. Above: Landscape near Bar-sur-Aube

THE VINEYARDS OF THE AUBE are cultivated mainly between the towns of Bar-sur-Seine and Bar-sur-Aube, about 40 kilometres east of the medieval city of Troyes and about 100 kilometres south of the Marne vineyards. The Aube vineyards are in fact part of Champagne, entitled to the same appellation, made from the same grapes and in the same way. However the region is very much the poor relation, and the most famous and respected champagne houses are all based around Reims in the more northerly vineyards of the Marne.

THE WINES

It is generally accepted that the wines produced in the Aube are of a lesser quality than those of its more illustrious neighbour, Champagne. At the end of the nineteenth century the vineyards of the Aube were badly affected by phylloxera, and the depleted vineyards became separated from those of the northern Champagne and excluded from the appellation. A succession of bad harvests and problems experienced in selling and transporting the Aube wines led many thousands of *vignerons* and their supporters to descend upon the city of Troyes in the spring of 1911 to protest at their exclusion. As a result the government redefined the limits of the appellation and gave them back their earlier status.

To some extent this reunion has not been entirely successful because the wines from the Reims region have retained their reputation for superiority and are much more widely exported. However, there is much of interest here for the wine lover, including some excellent champagne as well as interesting

Coteaux Champenois wines. Rosé des Riceys, for example, which Louis XIV was fond of, is a delightful deep pink, full-bodied rosé which is quite unusual and rarely found outside the region.

THE CUISINE

The food of the Aube is very similar to that of the Marne. The *charcuterie* is outstanding, particularly the *andouillettes* of Bar-sur-Aube and Bar-sur-Seine and the Troyes version which are made of mutton. There are some interesting local cheeses from the villages of Chaource (a light, creamy, cow's-milk cheese with an almost soufflé-like texture) and its neighbour Mussy (a cheese of similar appearance but with a firmer texture and slightly stronger flavour). Another cow's-milk cheese is produced in the village of Les Riceys and goes perfectly with a glass of Rosé des Riceys. *Fromage blanc*, a creamy mould of fresh cheese curd, is commonly served in many parts of France with sugar and

Above: A medieval house in Bar-sur-Aube
Left: A summer landscape near Bergères

cream as a dessert; I was given it in a small restaurant in the Aube served with salt, pepper, finely-minced garlic and a generous sprinkling of fresh herbs – absolutely delicious!

THE ROUTE DES VINS *Michelin maps 61 and 65*

If you are travelling from the north, you could visit the vineyards concentrated around the ancient town of Sézanne. These can be explored by taking a small road, the D453, along a gentle ridge of hills through the vineyards to the tiny wine villages of Vindey and Saudoy. The vineyards continue spasmodically as far as the market town of Villenauxe-la-Grande on the N51.

The regional park of La Forêt d'Orient, immediately to the north of the Route des Vins, is also worth a small detour. It is an extensive, dense forest, around a large lake. There are water-sport facilities at the lakeside village of

A distant view of Les Riceys

Wild flowers edging a field near St Usage

Mesnil-St-Père, or you can enjoy bird watching – and there are plenty of good spots for fishing and picnicking.

The Route des Vins in the Aube is quite well signposted and easy to follow. It is a complete circuit and so can be joined at any convenient place. But a good starting point is the charming town of Bar-sur-Seine, whose narrow streets are lined with medieval houses with timbered façades. The church of Saint Etienne dates from the sixteenth century. The Château des Comtes de Bar, with its unusual clock-tower, is set on a hill above the town and is well worth a visit.

Leave the town on the main road, the N 71, going towards Châtillon-sur-Seine (where the archaeological museum displays important Grecian artefacts found locally). After a kilometre or so you'll come to a small road on the left that leads to the wine village of Merrey-sur-Arce, which has some old houses typical of the region. Continuing on the D 167, you come to the village of Celles-sur-Ource, where there are some important wine establishments whose wines you can sample and buy. The countryside here is quite open with gentle hills, meadows and fields of maize, wheat and barley; the vineyards are confined mainly to the tops and slopes of the slight hills.

After crossing the N 71, take a quiet country road, the D 452, to the village of Polisy at the confluence of the Seine and Laignes rivers. It is a sombre place made up of some rather austere old stone houses, a gloomy sixteenth-century château and a church containing an interesting Virgin and Child and some fine murals. The wine route continues to the hamlet of Balnot-sur-Laignes, which is known for its red and rosé Coteaux Champenois wines, set at the head of a valley. Here the Route des Vins climbs along the side of the valley into the wood of Riceys. A left turn on to the D 142 takes you to the top of a steep hill; from here you can see Les Riceys, a village where the vines are quite extensively cultivated.

Les Riceys is in fact three villages in one. The first you encounter is Ricey-Bas, which has an elegant Renaissance church beside the river Laignes. Nearby is a château, the oldest parts of which date back to the eleventh century. A little further along the road, virtually merged, are Ricey-Haut and Ricey-Haut-Rive, both with distinctive churches. There are several places where you can taste and buy the local Rosé des Riceys and champagne.

A village house in Baroville

Previous pages: The river Caignes. Above: Near Fontette

Return to Ricey-Bas, and continue on the wine route along the D 70, crossing the N 71, to the village of Gyé-sur-Seine, which has a twelfth-century church and the remains of a fourteenth-century château. From here, you can make a small detour to Neuville-sur-Seine, which has a *cave co-opérative* and is dominated by a statue of Nôtre Dame des Vignes set on the top of the hill above the village. Now this is the perfect place to lie in the long grass with a *baguette*, a piece of Chaource and a bottle of Rosé des Riceys, and allow the cares of the world to pass you by.

Follow the Route des Vins through a peaceful little valley along the D 103 to Loches-sur-Ource, then cross its Roman bridge and turn on to the D 67 to Essoyes, through which the River Ource meanders. The great Impressionist painter, Pierre-Auguste Renoir, his wife and two famous sons – actor Pierre and film-maker Jean – are buried in the churchyard. The house they lived in between 1897 and 1916 is on the edge of the town, marked with a plaque, and there are plans to open a *maison du vin* here.

There are fine views over the vineyards as the Route des Vins continues along the D 70 to the village of Fontette; there is a *cave co-opérative* here. Just before the next village, St Usage, there is a detour to the high point of the downs giving some breathtaking panoramas over the plateau of Blu. Then on to Champignol-lez-Mondeville, a small village set in a wide valley and surrounded by cornfields, meadows, vineyards and fields of sunflowers. The wine road now continues along the D 101A to Arconville and then to Baroville, where there is a *cave co-opérative*. Continuing along the D 396 you come to Bayel, where you can visit the famous crystal glass works, La

The endless horizons, typical of the Aube region, near Bergères

Cristallerie de Champagne; they have a shop selling the crystal.

The Route des Vins follows the D 47 to Lignol-le-Château, at the crossroads with the N 19. There are two twelfth-century buildings here – a church and a château. You can make a detour to the village of Colombey-les-Deux-Eglises, where Charles de Gaulle lived; he is buried in the local cemetery. The next village is Rouvres-les-Vignes, then Colombé-le-Sec, where there is an important *cave co-opérative*. Nearby are the ancient cellars of the Abbaye de Clairvaux; these date back to the twelfth century and can be visited.

Go through the small village of Colombé-la-Fosse to Arrentières, where there are remains of a fourteenth-century castle; it was demolished on the orders of Louis XIII. From here the Route des Vins continues to the bustling market town of Bar-sur-Aube. This ancient town has a number of medieval buildings with timbered façades, an Hôtel de Ville of the seventeenth-century, and the twelfth-century Eglise de St Pierre whose striking interior includes a wooden gallery. There is a wine-tasting chalet on the outskirts of the town beside the N 19 in the direction of Chaumont.

The route back towards Bar-sur-Seine starts off along the D 4 towards Proverville. Shortly after leaving the town you take a small road to the left to the chapel of Sainte Germaine, set high on the hill above the town and offering splendid views of the valley of the Aube. A delightfully scenic road completes the circuit back to Bar-sur-Seine, passing through a succession of small wine villages such as Meurville, with its twelfth-century church and Ville-sur-Arce, where there is the *cave co-opérative* of the Coteaux de l'Arce.

A Tour of Alsace

Left: The Black Forest from Haut Konigsburg. Above: Vineyards near Dieffenthal

ORDERS ARE MADE to be disputed, as every student of Alsatian history knows. France's easternmost province has been passed from one régime and ruler to another and back again for thousands of years, from the Celts to the Romans to the Franks and their Merovingian kings. Then there were 700 years of German rule from the tenth century – and a legacy of fine Renaissance architecture remains. The peace and prosperity were followed by several centuries of war, during which time the region was thrown back and forward between France and Germany. Its present status as French dates from the Treaty of Versailles after the 1914–18 War.

Alsace's landscape is as dramatic as its history: the rugged Vosges mountains with their wooded slopes extend for almost 160 kilometres north to south, running parallel to the River Rhine. Within this domain are crystal-clear lakes, woodland walks, fairy-tale villages and, of course, the vineyards. These are concentrated on the foothills of the Vosges and stretch from the village of Nordheim, near Strasbourg, in the north to Thann, west of Mulhouse, in the south. Understandably, there is a strong German feel to the wines of Alsace, as in its art, architecture, cuisine and landscape.

THE WINES

The wine of Alsace is predominantly white and, unlike the wines of other regions, is identified primarily by grape type. The main varieties are Sylvaner, Muscat, Riesling, Tokay–Pinot Gris, Gewürztraminer, Pinot Blanc and Pinot Noir from which red and rosé wines are made. In addition, there is a wine called Edelzwicker, which is a blend of various grape types, including the

Previous pages: Near Itterswiller. Above: Harvesting near Marlenheim

Chasselas; Edelzwicker is the basic, everyday wine of the region, often served in restaurants in the traditional blue-and-white earthenware jug.

THE CUISINE

The freshly grown produce of Alsace is magnificent: there is a rich variety of grain, vegetable and fruit grown in the fertile Rhine Valley, the lakes and mountains of the Vosges ensure a good supply of fish, while game, beef and dairy products from the mountain meadows and valleys are also abundant.

One of the most famous dishes – and a truly hearty feast – is of course *choucroute Alsacienne*; it is made of sauerkraut and potato and served with a variety of meats including salt pork, smoked ham and sausages. (Incidentally, you can follow the Route de la Choucroute through the countryside where the cabbages are grown.) Another equally rich and substantial speciality is *baeckaoffa*, a delicious stew made with three types of meat, usually mutton, pork and beef. The pork is very good here: it is smoked, made into sausages, stewed, and eaten roasted with pickled turnips. Geese are raised to make the *terrines* and *pâtes de foie gras truffés* which rival those from Périgord. *Kugelhopf* is another regional speciality; it is a light, sweet, distinctively shaped *brioche*, flavoured with raisins and almonds and dusted with sugar.

A wine merchant's house in Eguisheim

Alsace also boasts one of the best – and strongest – cheeses in France: *Munster*. Made from the milk of the cows you see grazing just west of the town the cheese is named after, it is often served with a generous sprinkling of cumin seed and a glass of spicy Gewürztraminer wine.

One of the most renowned French restaurants, the Auberge de l'Ill at Illhaueserin, is close to the wine route. And you can enjoy the simple and informal *winstubs*, a cross between German beer kellers and wine bars, which offer good food and wine in cosy surroundings. The friendly Winstub Arnold in Itterswiller, overlooking the vineyards, is particularly worth visiting.

A winter landscape near Riquewihr

A vigneron *from Riquewihr*

Harvesting the grapes near Ottrott

T H E R O U T E D E S V I N S *Michelin maps 62 and 66*

Marlenheim on the busy N 4, a few miles west of Strasbourg, is where the Alsace Route des Vins starts. There are vineyards further north, around Wissembourg, but the main area to explore, and the well-signposted wine route proper, lies to the south of Marlenheim. This town is noted for its rosé wine, called Vorlauf, made from the Pinot Noir grape, and for the important wine festival it holds every September; and there are a number of attractive half-timbered houses near the Hôtel de Ville.

Leaving Marlenheim, the D 422 towards Wangen takes you on to the first leg of the official Route des Vins. Here on the rolling hills, you see vineyards side by side with fields of food crops and grazing cattle and sheep. The best time to visit this rich agricultural region is in late autumn when the harvest is taking place and the turning leaves create vivid bursts of colour, as the first dustings of snow cover the more exposed upper slopes of the Vosges. Although tiny tractors have taken the place of horses, the other traditional harvesting methods survive. The grapes are still collected in wooden barrel-like tubs and are loaded on to ancient wooden carts. The vineyards hum with excitement and it seems that the entire population is recruited to help. The narrow, cobbled village streets are constantly jammed with tractors

A distant view of the wine village of Andlau

towing cart-loads of grapes; drying tubs are stacked everywhere and the air is
heady with the smell of fermenting juice.

The Route des Vins meanders along a quiet country road that twists and
turns its way through several small villages to the west of the main road. This
region is known as the Bas-Rhin. The university town of Molsheim is situated
below the vine-clad Molsheimer Berg on the River Bruche. There is an
unusual sixteenth-century Renaissance building, the 'Metzig', which was
erected by the butchers' guild and now houses the museum. Obernai, an
important market town, has a sixteenth-century corn market and an Hôtel de
Ville, and you can look to the forests of Vosges from its medieval ramparts.

A little to the west is the small town of Ottrott, known for its rosé and red
wines; nearby Boersch is a slumbering old village with a fortified gateway,
many timbered houses and narrow cobbled streets. Barr, an important wine
centre, is the next large town on the route and nestles below a steep hill lined
with vines. It would make a good base from which to explore the northern part
of Alsace, especially in March when there is a wine fair centred around its
seventeenth-century château. Nearby is Mont Ste Odile, a hilltop convent
established by Alsace's patron saint, who is buried in the small twelfth-
century chapel; it is a spectacular viewpoint and a place of pilgrimage. Two
other villages not to be missed, within a short distance are Mittelbergheim
and Andlau; the latter is tucked into a niche in a steep-sided green valley. As
you follow the wine route a little further south you come to Itterswiller, a
welcoming little village perched on the edge of the vineyards, its single,
narrow street lined with houses that always seem to be decked with flowers.

The Vosges seen from the vineyards above Riquewihr

The next main town is Dambach-la-Ville, the home of a number of important growers; there are medieval ramparts, three fortified gates and a sixteenth-century town hall to see here as well. Continuing south the road leads you through the small villages of Orschwiller, St Hippolyte and Bergheim towards Ribeauvillé. Here the Vosges become more rugged and dramatic and the vineyards creep up the lower slopes. You can take a minor detour from Orschwiller up to the castle of Haut-Koenigsbourg; a small road winds up through beautiful woods to the summit of the mountain, from where you can see over the vineyards to the distant Rhine – on a clear day you can even see the Black Forest.

Ribeauvillé is known for its wines – Gewürztraminer and Riesling – and its music: on its annual feast day, the first Sunday in September, the fountain in the main square flows with wine, and there is a street festival of strolling musicians. Set in a narrow valley in the foothills of the Vosges, it is ringed with vineyards. The cobbled streets are lined with beautiful old timbered houses and you'll find many places to taste and buy the wines of local growers, as well as *charcuteries, pâtisseries* and *épiceries* to buy the regional culinary specialities. Nearby is the charming small village of Hunawihr, also well worth a visit.

Riquewihr, next on the route, is the pride and joy of Alsace – and undoubtedly one of the loveliest wine villages in France, if at times a little crowded, especially at the height of summer when busloads of tourists descend on it. It has everything a perfectly preserved, historical village should have; ramparts, fortified gates, fifteenth-century houses with sculp-

The vineyards which surround the village of Riquewihr

Kaysersberg seen from its ruined castle

Above: A conversation in Colmar. Following pages: Eguisheim

tured doorways, ornate balconies, wrought-iron signs, cobbled courtyards and winding narrow streets, all a blaze of floral colour. But it's not all show; there are many important growers based here, including Hugel and Dopff. Climb up beyond the village ramparts through the vineyards and look out over to the distant Vosges.

From Riquewihr the wine route continues through the small villages of Mittelwihr, Sigolsheim and Kientzheim to Kaysersberg, at the entrance to the Weiss Valley. This is where Albert Schweitzer was born in 1875. The town is dominated by a ruined castle, the streets are lined with medieval and sixteenth-century houses and there is a fifteenth-century fortified bridge incorporating a chapel. The next village is Turckheim, where, as in many other Alsatian villages, a platform has been built high up, usually around a church steeple or tower, in the hope that a pair of storks will build their nest on it; the stork is the local symbol for good luck.

Colmar is the centre of the Alsace wine trade and hosts an important wine fair in mid-August. It is a lovely town set on the River Lauch, with many important old buildings, including the Maison Pfister (a fine example of a carved wooden façade), l'Ancienne Douane (the old customs house) and a medieval guard house. The museum of Unterlinden, in a thirteenth-century Dominican monastery, houses an extensive collection of medieval religious art; the showpiece, though, is Mathias Grünewald's Issenheim altar piece, a superb example of German Renaissance art, and there are works by Picasso and Braque in the modern galleries downstairs. The museum also contains a section on the local wine history: it is a colourful past centred around the

Above: A local farmer
Right: The ruined towers of Husseren-les-
Château stand guard over the vineyards

poêles, private drinking clubs whose exclusive membership demanded exclusive – and excellent – wines. There is a lively weekly market in the old central square, where the local farmers sell their produce, and there are many wine-growers' establishments where the regional wines can be found. Colmar has a number of excellent restaurants, *winstubs*, and hotels too; it is a good base from which to explore the surrounding vineyards and villages.

Continuing south the Route des Vins leads you to Eguisheim, an Alsatian village which has changed little since the sixteenth century. Its cobbled circular street, which runs around the inside of the rampart walls, is lined with lovely old houses and courtyards. There is a very good *cave co-opérative* here which sells an unusual sparkling Blanc de Blancs as well as the more familiar wines of the region; you can eat Alsatian specialities, such as *saucisse de Strasbourg*, at its restaurant as you sample the local wines.

Further south along the wine road is the village of Husseren-les-Châteaux; the ruins of three châteaux can be seen in the hills to the west overlooking the town. The next villages are Gueberschwihr, Soultzmatt, Bergholtzzell and Guebwiller, the latter at the entrance to the lovely Florival Valley. Near Soultzmatt are the highest vineyards in Alsace, known as the Zinkoepfle. The landscape here is dominated by the Grand Ballon, the highest peak of the Vosges at 1,400 metres.

The town of Thann marks the southern limit of the Alsace vineyards. From here, it's worth travelling a little further west into the Vosges, following the Route des Crêtes, to explore the lakes and forests. There are places here – Gérardmer, le Lac Vert, le Lac Blanc and le Lac Noir, for instance – that seem a world away from the nearby vineyards. They add yet another perspective to this unusual and much disputed corner of France.

A Case For Tasting

ALSACE WINES LOOK AND SOUND GERMAN. They come in slim, green *flûte* bottles similar to Mosels, and are always labelled with the names of their constituent grape variety – such as the Teutonic-sounding Riesling or Gewürztraminer. But Alsace wines are emphatically French – dry and excitingly flavoured, ideal for drinking with meals – and a delight to discover.

RIESLING HUGEL

The noble Riesling grape, backbone of all the best medium-sweet wines made over the border in Germany, makes for a very different wine in Alsace. Here top-quality Rieslings such as Hugel's Réserve Personelle are dry, yet with exquisite intensity of grapey flavour, and best after five years' ageing. 90FF.

DOPFF SCHOENENBURG RIESLING

The Riquewihr firm of Dopff Au Moulin's vineyard at Schoenenburg – one of forty-eight prime hillside sites designated *Grands Crus* – makes a Riesling of keen freshness and delicate fruitiness, especially in a great vintage such as 1985 (together with 1983, the best of the decade). Wonderful with fish. 60FF.

ZIND-HUMBRECHT BRAND RIESLING

This is a *vendange-tardive* – 'late-harvest' – wine from grapes picked in a sunny autumn some weeks after the main harvest and thus riper than normal. The resulting wine, from Zind-Humbrecht's vineyard in the Brand *Grand Cru*, is dry but with weighty concentration of flavour and a lovely golden colour. 150FF.

KUENTZ-BAS GEWÜRZTRAMINER

Alsace Gewürztraminer is the region's most distinctive wine, with a pungent grapey aroma and thrillingly intense, spicy dry flavour to go with its crystal-gold colour. Kuentz-Bas, a small family firm also revered for other great wines, makes a Gewürz with beautifully defined flavour. 50FF.

DOPFF GEWÜRZTRAMINER

Sélection de Grains Nobles signifies a wine made from individually selected grapes which have ripened to the extent of 'noble' rottenness and a raisiny concentration of flavour. Dopff's extraordinary, deep-gold, lingeringly delicious wine is a *vin de garde* ready to drink from the late 1990s onwards. 300FF.

CHARLES SCHLÉRET SYLVANER

In Alsace, the Sylvaner makes a fresh and clean-tasting dry white wine with a grassy aroma and flavour. Light and crisp though the best examples are, their taste is positive enough to make Sylvaners a good accompaniment to rich Alsace dishes. The talented Charles Schléret makes an excellent wine. 30FF.

TRIMBACH PINOT BLANC

The Pinot Blanc grape makes a lightweight but fully fruity dry white in Alsace. This one, from the major Ribeauvillé firm of Trimbach – run today by the eleventh successive generation of the family – is very fresh and easy to drink, either as an apéritif or with a light meal. 30FF.

SCHLUMBERGER PINOT GRIS

Also known as the Tokay d'Alsace, the Pinot Gris grape is characterised by wine with a powerful aroma, weighty body and rich, heady flavour. Schlumberger's Réserve Spéciale is very full, with a fine smoky smell and flavour. A wine to drink no sooner than five years after the vintage, and good with rich food. 60FF.

MURÉ TOKAY-PINOT GRIS

Clos St Landelin is the proverbial south-facing slope – in this case, Muré's wonderful, sun-baked hillside vineyard in the *Grand Cru* of Vorbourg. This spectacular wine is a *Sélection de Grains Nobles* (see Dopff Gewürztraminer) from 1983: golden, honeyed, unforgettable. 280FF.

MUSCAT HUGEL

Elsewhere in France, the Muscat grape makes sweet wine. In Alsace, Muscat is enticingly sweet to smell, but quite dry in flavour, delicately spicy and light. Hugel say of their Cuvée Tradition that it 'gives the sensation of biting into fresh Muscat grapes'. Very fair comment. 50FF.

LAUGEL CRÉMANT D'ALSACE

Made by the Champagne method, Alsace *Crémant* (creamily sparkling) wines are serious rivals to all sparklers bar champagne itself. Laugel's wine, from the Pinot Blanc grape, is light but deeply flavoured, finely balanced between fruitiness and freshness, with a fine, persistent froth. 40FF.

LEON BEYER ROUGE D'ALSACE

In Alsace, the Pinot Noir makes a truly elegant dry red wine – the region's only red. Leon Béyer's wine is light in body with the raspberry aroma that characterizes the grape. 40FF. An outstanding Pinot Noir is Kuentz-Bas Réserve Personelle, deep-coloured, rich and gloriously scented, to drink at five or more years old. 50FF.

A Tour of the Jura

The vineyards of Château Chalon

RIVING SOUTH on the N 83 from Besançon, you will get your first glimpse of the Jura vineyards a few kilometres north of the town of Arbois, where the rolling hills that signal the approach of the Jura plateau also define the eastern border of the plain of Bresse.

The wines of the Jura have long been regarded with respect. Pliny mentioned them, and they were greatly appreciated by the Romans. They have also graced the tables of many discerning people from the dukes of Burgundy to Rabelais and Brillat-Savarin, the French writer and gastronome. The soil on which the vines are grown is a mixture of limestone often combined with clay, the subsoil being a compacted marl. In the Arbois area the land has a crust of aalian limestone on a foundation of lias, sand and marl which is particularly favourable to the Savagnin and Poulsard grapes. Vine cultivation is hard work in the Jura; many of the vines are planted on terraces cut into the steep hillsides and when the soil is washed down, as often happens during heavy rainfalls, it must be carried back to the vineyards.

THE WINES

Among the grape varieties grown here are the Ploussard (or Poulsard) from which rosé wines are made, the Trousseau from which red wine is made, the Savagnin, from which the renowned *vin jaune* is made, and the Chardonnay for fine white wines that can be kept for many years. Both the Poulsard and Trousseau and the Chardonnay and Savagnin are often blended during harvesting to produce wines with a considerable variety of colour, from very pale gold through yellow, amber and light pink to rich ruby.

For such a relatively small area, the Jura produces an amazing variety of wine. The regional speciality, *vin jaune*, is made by an unusual method, shared by the Spanish Jerez wines. The Savagnin grapes are harvested late, often not until November, and are pressed in the same way as for a conventional white wine, but the juice is then put in barrels and kept for up to ten years (six is the legal minimum). During this period a veil of yeasts develops on its surface, the wine begins to oxidize, creating the characteristic deep yellow colour and at the same time a subtle and unusual bouquet and flavour develop, often compared to hazelnuts. The exact nature of this transition is not fully understood, nor can it be totally controlled. The natural loss of wine from evaporation in the cask (ullage) is not made up as with normal wines during ageing, and this makes good *vin jaune* a rather expensive and relatively rare commodity. It goes very well served at room temperature with the local Comté cheese, and is also drunk chilled as an apéritif.

*Above and left: Vineyards in summer near
the village of Toulouse-le-Château*

Another unusual wine for which the Jura is famous is *vin de paille*, or straw
wine, so called because the grapes are dried on a bed of straw for three months
before pressing. This produces a sweet,highly alcoholic dessert wine which
compares favourably with a Sauternes; it can be kept for fifty years or more.
Sparkling wines are also produced in the Jura and Henri Maire extols the
virtues of his *vin fou*, or mad wine, on hoardings throughout France.

Of the other wines the rosés are of particular interest and are as highly
rated as the well-known Rhône wine Tavel. Most rosé wines are left only
briefly in contact with the skins of the black grapes to give them colour. But
the Poulsard grapes of the Jura have less pigmentation than other varieties,
and this means that the juice and skins can be left to ferment together for
many days, as they would for a red wine, without losing the delicacy of colour
expected of rosé. This gives the Jura rosés well-defined body and flavour and
the ability to be kept for longer than most other rosés.

A village house in Pupillin

THE CUISINE

The trout, perch, pike (*brochet*) and carp from the Jura's rivers are excellent, and there is plenty of game found in its forests and hills, including hare, pigeon, woodcock (*bécasse*) and pheasant, which are used to produce some intriguing pâtés and *terrines*. You can find the local smoked hams and *andouillettes* in every *charcuterie*. The dish you will experience most frequently is *coq au vin jaune*, a delicious concoction of chicken in a rich but light sauce made with cream and *vin jaune* and thickened with egg yolks; in spring it is served with *morels*, dark brown wild fungi which have a quite subtle flavour.

The brown and white cows that graze on the hillsides and meadows provide milk for the region's cheeses. These include the famous Comté, much of which is produced in co-opératives – many of the individual herds are quite small and Comté is a very large cheese! At one small co-opérative in a hill-town above Salins-les-Bains, the proprietor showed me the vast copper vats holding over 1,000 litres of milk which, she explained, is made into two cheeses weighing about 45 kilos each.

THE ROUTE DES VINS *Michelin Map 70*

There is no signposted Route des Vins leading through the Jura but the route I suggest will take you through the most satisfying countryside and the most important vineyards and villages. Although most of the vineyards are contained within a narrow strip of land, rarely more than about 5 kilometres wide, between Arbois in the north and St Amour in the south alongside the N 83, it is possible to tour the vineyards all day and hardly be aware that the

Above: Near Salins-les-Bains. Following pages: The Cirque de Baume

main road is so near. While the Jura mountains are neither as lofty nor as imposing as the Alps to the south, they nevertheless offer some dramatic and spectacular scenery, particularly on the fissured rim of the plateau, where the rock is broken by precipitous gorges and plunging ravines.

Just north of Arbois and to the east of the N 83, in the valley of the River Furieuse, lies the thermal spa of Salins-les-Bains. This is a good starting point for a tour through the wine-growing area of the Jura. To reach the town, leave the N 83 a little way north of Arbois; if time allows, make several stops before you get there. Port-Lesney, to the west of the main road on the banks of the river Loue, offers a peaceful retreat for anglers and campers and there are walks along the river and through the surrounding woods. The village of les Arsures, just north of Arbois, is also worth a visit, not only to try its fine wine but also for the seclusion of its quiet lanes and vine-clad hills. I passed a memorable hour here in a meadow just a few hundred metres from the main road, watching a pair of kestrels riding the thermals above my head, with a simple picnic of bread, Morbier cheese and a good bottle of Arbois red wine.

The N 83 takes you right into the centre of Arbois; there are many wine growers around the Place de la Liberté selling their products, and the town's Fruitière Vinicole (the name for the wine co-operatives of the region) is here too. Just along the main street is the imposing Les Deux Tonneaux, owned by Henri Maire, a grower whose wines are known throughout France. Nearby, in a small street behind the Hôtel de Ville, is the recently established wine museum. Try to plan your visit to Arbois to coincide with one of the most spectacular harvest festivals in France, the *Fête de Biou*, which is held in the

The ancient roofs of Arbois

Vineyards near Château Chalon

The cave-co-opérative *in Arbois*

streets here on the first Sunday in September; the high point of the festival is when about 100 kilogrammes of grapes are carried in procession through the town to the church. Arbois was the boyhood home of Louis Pasteur; the house he lived in on the bank of the River Cuisance is still there. He did much of his experimental work into fermentation and wine-making at a small vineyard in les Rosières, just north of Arbois.

Continue south from Arbois on the D 246, climbing into the foothills of the Jura towards the little village of Pupillin, which is said to make the best red wine of the region. Here you really know that you are in mountain country, although it is only a few hundred metres above Arbois. Even at the height of summer, there are massive piles of wood stacked against every house in readiness for the cold, dark evenings ahead. And, as if in defiance of the rigours of mountain life, every house will be ablaze with bright geraniums and petunias adorning all available corners and ledges, soaking up every ounce of the summer's warmth and colour as an antidote to the oncoming winter. It was up here in the mountains that an old *vigneron* explained to me that the Jura vines are among the purest strains in France; only grapes of noble lineage are grown and, he added, if necessary, vineyards are compulsorily uprooted in order to maintain this tradition.

From Pupillin the D 246 rejoins the N 83. Follow this a short distance until you get to the fortified village of Poligny, which is an important wine centre; many growers have establishments in its narrow streets and the Fruitière Vinicole (called the Caveau des Jacobins) is situated in an old church. There are many buildings of architectural interest here, including the seventeenth-

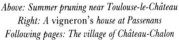

Above: Summer pruning near Toulouse-le-Château
Right: A vigneron's *house at Passenans*
Following pages: The village of Château-Chalon

century Ursuline convent and the Hotel Dieu with its vaulted halls and kitchens and old pharmacy; there is a superb collection of Burgundian documents in the Church of St-Hippolyte. A few kilometres from Poligny, towards Champagnole, is the beautiful and dramatic wooded gorge at Vaux, from which you have fine views over the surrounding countryside.

A little way further south from Poligny along the N 83 turn left on to the quiet D 57 towards St Lothain, and you will come to a succession of charming villages, including Passenans, Frontenay, Menétru-le-Vignoble and Domblans. You will be able to taste the local wines as you go. This area is known as the Revermont, literally 'the back of the mountain', and some of the more dramatic scenery – wide rolling landscapes with distant views of mountains, sudden surging hills and abrupt escarpments – can be seen at Château-Chalon, a village famed for its Vin Jaune, which is perched on a 460-metre

A Case For Tasting

THE WINES OF THE JURA are highly distinctive. Most famous is the ageless *vin jaune*, made in a way that gives it close similarities to sherry. Other wines of the region share *vin jaune*'s characteristics of intensity and earthy flavour. They are an acquired taste – but well made, and very well worth discovering.

CENDRÉ VIN GRIS HENRI MAIRE

'Grey' wine is in fact pale rosé. Jura *vin gris* is noted for its crisp, clean sharpness and makes a lively, palate-stimulating apéritif. Henri Maire's Cendré is a good example, fruity but with a refreshingly keen acidity, to drink chilled either on its own or, says Henri Maire, with just about every kind of food. 20FF.

VIN JAUNE CHÂTEAU DE L'ETOIL

The l'Etoile *appellation*, named after the village – so-called because of the star-shaped fossils common in the area – makes small quantities of *vin jaune*. Château de l'Etoile's wine comes in a 62cl *clavelin* bottle, as does all *vin jaune*, and will, they say, 'conserve its virtues and aroma for more than a century'! 100FF.

CHÂTEAU CHALON JEAN BOURDY

The tiny (sixty acres) Château Chalon *appellation* makes the most acclaimed *vin jaune* of the Jura. The wine is made from very ripe Savagnin grapes and aged in oak barrels for at least six years, becoming distinctly like dry sherry. Jean Bourdy's wine is powerfully scented, rich, and very dry. 150FF.

CHÂTEAU DE L'ETOILE MÉTHODE CHAMPENOISE

Sparkling wines from the Jura have shown marked improvements in recent years. The same grapes that go into champagne itself, Chardonnay and Pinot Noir, are used – as is the laborious, but rewarding, 'champagne method' of production. Château de l'Etoile *brut* is keenly fresh with a lively *mousse*. 30FF

ARBOIS BLANC DOMAINE DE GRANGE GRILLARD

Centre of the Jura, the town of Arbois gives its name to the region's best-known *appellation controlée*. White Arbois is yellow-gold in colour, intense, almost sherry-like in flavour, and completely dry. Grange Grillard, from Arbois' leading winemaker Henri Maire, is almondy and delicious. 60FF.

MACVIN CHÂTEAU DE L'ETOILE

This is the Jura's answer to Champagne's Ratafia and Cognac's Pineau des Charentes – unfermented grape juice spiked with spirit. Macvin, or Marc-vin, is sweet juice blended with Jura *marc* – a distillation of local grapes, aged at least two years in oak casks. L'Etoile's version is a sweet, potent apéritif. 50FF.

CÔTES DU JURA ROSÉ CHÂTEAU DE L'ETOILE

This is the basic rosé of the region, made from a mix of Pinot Noir, Poulsard and Trousseau grapes. Château de l'Etoile's wine has a fine browny-pink colour and delicate, subtle aroma; the taste is dry and delicate, too. L'Etoile recommend drinking it *très frais* – well-chilled. 30FF.

BONCHALAZ HENRI MAIRE

By far the biggest and best-known of Jura winemakers, Henri Maire makes numerous branded wines as well as traditional *appellations*. Bonchalaz is a light, slightly sweet red *vin de table*. 'The ideal companion', says Maire, 'to all delightful dishes in the rural tradition'. 20FF.

CÔTES DU JURA ROUGE JEAN BOURDY

Made, like the rosé wines of the region, with varying mixes of Pinot Noir, Poulsard and Trousseau grapes, Jura reds are typically light and quite dry. Jean Bourdy's wine has, he says, 'an original character with a very pronounced *gout de terroir* (flavour of the land)'. Best with roast meat. 30FF.

VIN DE PAILLE JEAN BOURDY

'Straw wine' is so known because the grapes for it are spread out on mats – traditionally of straw – to dry out for several weeks after the harvest. They thus become very concentrated in natural sugar, and ultimately, after long fermentation, make very sweet wine, such as Jean Bourdy's. Drink chilled, with a pudding. 150FF.

CHÂTEAU D'ARLAY

Like all *vin jaune*, Château D'Arlay's wine improves with decanting – preferably several hours in advance. Arlay commend the wine as an accompaniment to Comté cheese, *foie gras truffé de canard*, crayfish, *coq au vin*, even caviare. *Vin jaune* is traditionally served at room temperature. 120FF.

COTES DU JURA BLANC CHÂTEAU D'ARLAY

As in Arbois, the Côtes du Jura *AC* makes white wines yellow in colour, intense and nutty in flavour. The same grape varieties, Chardonnay, Pinot Blanc and Savagnin, are used. Château D'Arlay's wine is dry and, rightly, billed as 'marked by the aromas and flavours of nuts and dried fruits'. 50FF.

Wine-buying Guide

CHAMPAGNE

This is a region with a fascinating history and outstanding wine, although the scenery is less interesting. The wine is mostly sold not by geographical district but as one appellation – Champagne. It is marketed as a blended wine by the brand name of the champagne house that produces it.

Blending is the true art of champagne making. Far from being a technique of mixing indifferent and better quality wine to elevate the general mixture (*coupage*), here blending is an art – *assemblage*. This is the building of a complete picture from individual constituent wines. The best analogy is to regard a single unblended wine as a monochromatic picture and compare it with an *assemblage* of wines as a full-colour picture.

The opportunities to buy the wine are manifold, making advice surprisingly difficult to give. The big companies, mostly centred around Reims, Epernay and Ay, all have efficient publicity departments. They have well-known names and are called the *grandes marques*. They are the significant firms in the champagne export market. Each *grande marque* will take you on a tour of their cavernous cellars, show you large-scale production of champagne, and give you an opportunity to taste and buy.

These are the *grandes marques*, town by town. In Ay: Ayala, Bollinger, Deutz and Gelderman. In Epernay: Moët et Chandon, Perrier-Jouet and Pol Roger. In Reims: Besserat de Belleton (owned by the Pernod/Ricard group), Canard Duchêne (owned by Veuve Clicquot), George Goulet, Heidsieck Monopole, Charles Heidsieck (in the Henriot group), Henriot (owned by Veuve Clicquot) Krug, Lanson Père et Fils (under the same ownership as Pommery et Greno), Mercier (owned by the Moët-Hennessy group), G H Mumm (owned by Seagrams), Piper-Heidsieck, Pommery et Greno, Louis Roederer, Ruinart Père et Fils (also owned by the Moët-Hennessy group), Taittinger and Veuve Clicquot-Ponsardin. Finally, in Tours-sur-Marne: Laurent-Perrier.

Companies called *Marque Acheteur* or BOB (buyer's own brand) also market champagne. They are often as big as Grande Marque companies, and are occasionally subsidiaries of them. They make champagne to be sold under a company's own label and all supermarket, department store, and other such brand-name champagnes are made by these firms. They tend not to sell champagne under their own names.

In complete contrast there are the smaller *récoltants-manipulants*. These are small growers who make unblended wine from their own vineyards and sell direct to the local domestic markets. There are also *négociants-manipulants*. These are usually fairly small firms which own few,

if any, vineyards. They blend the products of different vineyards over a limited locality, often swapping with the more prestigious houses their quality first pressing (*première cuvée*) juice for double the quantity of lesser (*taille*) juice.

Of 5,000 champagne producers, only 127 produce more than 50,000 bottles a year (1981 figures).

THE CRU CLASSIFICATION SYSTEM

Champagne has a rather peculiar classification system based on vineyard geography, grape variety and price. Of the three main sub-districts of Champagne, the Montagne de Reims tends to grow the Pinot Noir; the Côte des Blancs grows the Chardonnay and the Vallée de la Marne grows the more robust yet less noble Pinot Meunier. The twelve village communes rated as *Grand Cru* are more concentrated in the Montagne de Reims and the Côte des Blancs because the Pinot Noir and the Chardonnay are the nobler, finer varieties. The price of each of these grapes is fixed annually, at harvest time, at a meeting between growers' and brokers' representatives, under the supervision of the *préfet* of the Marne *département*. The price is set by market pressure, stocks available in the cellars and the size of the harvest, and can fluctuate wildly from year to year.

The *Grand Cru* vineyard grapes fetch 100 per cent of this fixed price per kilo. The *Premiers Crus* fetch from 99 per cent down to 90

Harvesting the grapes near Boersch

per cent, and the lesser vineyards accordingly down to a minimum of 80 per cent (formerly 77 per cent). So vineyards can be classified in terms of a percentage relating to their grape prices.

WHAT ARE YOU BUYING?

The champagne produced by *grande marque* firms is substantially more expensive than that of the smaller *négociants* and growers because they tend to own or buy in grapes from the better classified vineyards. All *grandes marques* buy in grapes from contract growers because even the biggest, Moët et Chandon, only owns enough vineyards to satisfy a quarter to half of its requirements. In a *grande marque* blend the average classification of the grapes is usually about 97 per

cent. Also, when pressing the grapes, the *grandes marques* usually sell off the lesser quality *taille* pressings and only use the *cuvée* juice from the first pressing. Finally, they take a great deal of extra care during production and tend to age the constituent wines of a blend for longer than the legally required minimum for each category of champagne.

This, however, does not preclude the possibility of finding an exceptionally good growers' wine.

STYLES

De-luxe or *Cuvées de Prestige* Most *grandes marques* produce limited quantities of a de-luxe champagne *cuvée* from their best grapes. Exotic packaging and the quality of the wines in the blend add to the price. The styles vary from fragrant and delicate to rich and full according to the house style. By and large these wines tend to be of a single vintage.

Vintage Only five or six years in a decade are generally sufficiently good for making a vintage wine. A vintage champagne is a wine of a single year, although under AC

only produce thin, tart wines. By blending several years' grapes together, from good to less good, some more mature, some less mature, makers can produce a more balanced wine. The art of blending also allows for consistency in style and quality, year in and year out; a consistency that customers can rely on and that enables a firm's reputation as a brand to be built.

Non-vintage champagne is legally required to have a minimum of two years' ageing.

Crémant is a sparkling wine with two thirds of the fizziness of normal *méthode champenoise* wines. The term can be applied to vintage or non-vintage sparkling wine, with all the sweet/dry designations. A good one is Mumm's Crémant de Cramant, a Blanc de Blancs from the single *Grand Cru* village of Cramant.

SWEETNESS/DRYNESS DESIGNATIONS

All champagne is made dry. The sweetness is added at the final stage by putting in a percentage (by volume) of a sugar solution in wine. It is up to each firm to decide what percentage of sugar solution is given to each designation but the following is a guide:

Brut Zero or Brut Sauvage	0%
(Popular with dieters and diabetics, but fairly astringent.)	
Brut	1–2%
Extra Sec or Extra Dry	2–2½%
Sec	2½–4%
Demi-sec	4–6%
Doux or Rich	over 6%

COTEAUX CHAMPENOIS AC

As well as the more famous sparkling white and rosé, you must not forget the still wines that can be red, white or rosé in colour. Although now produced in relatively small quantities, it was these wines that made Champagne a widely known quality appellation prior to the advent of sparkling wines around the turn of the 17th Century.

Some is sold as Coteaux Champenois, but the best red comes from individual communes such as Bouzy. The whites are more common and Moët's Saran Nature and Ruinart's Chardonnay Blanc de Blancs are among the best but, although interesting, these wines will never be as great as the best white burgundies.

THE AUBE

The Aube is the fourth district within the appellation Champagne. While most champagne purists tend to ignore this sub-district, you should bear in mind that it accounts for 5,500 of the 27,000 hectares of the champagne vineyards. The wines produced here will never match the quality of those of the Montagne de Reims and the Côte des Blancs, but they are much in demand as less expensive champagnes.

LES RICEYS

To find and taste the Rosé des Riceys would broaden any amateur's appreciation of wine as it is extremely rare. The red also exists but it is the rosé (both come from the Pinot Noir grape) that, despite its delicacy, can age gracefully.

law the admixture of up to 10 per cent of another year is permitted. The wine produced typifies the style of the particular year and so, again, can range from light and delicate to full in taste. Vintage champagne will, of course, be a blend of wines from different village communes, but all of the same year. Wines of richer years can take on ten years of bottle age to arrive at a more complex character. Vintage champagne is legally required to have a minimum of three years' ageing.

Non-vintage These are wines made from a blend of grapes of more than one year. Because the champagne vineyards are so northerly, in some years the grapes do not fully ripen and can

ALSACE

This wine region is divided into two halves in the *départements* of Haut-Rhin and Bas-Rhin. The Haut-Rhin, to the south but higher up the Rhine valley, surprisingly produces the better wine. There is only one appellation – Alsace – which has 11,500 hectares of vineyards scattered on the slopes of the foothills of the Vosges. The wines are of an exceptional quality and it is sad that they are not more widely known and appreciated.

Harvesting 'buckets' en route

The wines are sold, not by geographical area, but under the appellation Alsace, followed by the grape variety. The only blend of varieties is Edelzwicker, made from the less noble Chasselas grape with a mixture of the more noble varieties. This is Alsace's 'jug' wine.

Since 1975 one superior appellation, Alsace Grand Cru, has existed. This is confined to 48 vineyard sites that have been known for generations to produce good wines. The name of the *Grand Cru* site may appear on the label and is geographically delimited. These *Grand Cru* wines have to be produced from the lower legal yield of 70 hectolitres per hectare, as opposed to the normal 100 hectos/hectare for Alsace. However, to complicate the picture, it is quite legal to put an individual vineyard name on a label if a wine is genuinely from a single vineyard, even if this vineyard is not a *Grand Cru*.

As the wines are sold without geographical delimitation within the appellation (*Grands Crus* aside), the trick is to buy either from specialists in particular grape varieties or from a firm recognized as thoroughly reliable.

TYPES OF MERCHANT IN ALSACE
Most of the better houses have been established for many years, some even since the 17th Century. These houses may own some vineyard holdings, but they invariably buy in grapes from smaller growers. Here are some of the firms with the name of their village: Léon Beyer (Eguisheim), E. Boekel (Mittelbergheim), Dopff et Irion (Riquewihr), Dopff au Moulin (Riquewihr), Theo Faller (Kayserberg), Heim (Westhalten), Hugel (Riquewihr), Kuentz-Bas (Husseren-les-Châteaux), Gustave Lorentz (Bergheim), Mure (Rouffach), J. Preiss-Zimmer (Riquewihr), F. E. Trimbach (Ribeauvillé).

Fewer than a third of the 9,200 producers own even one hectare of vineyard, so there are a great many very small growers. These growers form themselves into local co-operatives and pool their resources. This means that small operators do not have to provide all the capital for wine-making equipment themselves, but it does tend to produce less individual wines.

Village co-operatives include: Bennwihr, Dambach-la-Ville, Eguisheim and Ingersheim et Environs.

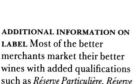

ADDITIONAL INFORMATION ON LABEL Most of the better merchants market their better wines with added qualifications such as *Réserve Particulière, Réserve Personelle, Cuvée Spéciale*, or *Cuvée Exceptionelle*; all variations on the same theme. However, these designations are copied by lesser merchants and so are rather meaningless.

Another distinction is *Vendange Tardive*. This covers wines made from grapes picked two or three weeks after normal harvesting. These wines are expensive because of the risk of heavy loss through frost or bad weather. In exceptional years, however, the extra autumn ripening produces wines of great richness and depth that are slightly sweeter than usual in style and can take years to develop fully in bottle.

EAUX-DE-VIE
Alsace is a great fruit-growing region and makes some of the finest *eaux-de-vie*. Common ones include Poire William from pear and Fraise from strawberry, and there are more exotic ones too,

from holly-berry, sorb-apple and cherry, that are well worth finding.

TASTING
It is important to taste Alsace wines, from the plainest and driest to the more aromatic styles. The following order of tasting is recommended: Sylvaner, Pinot Blanc, Tokay (also called Pinot Gris), Riesling, Muscat and finally Gewürztraminer. Taste any *Vendange Tardive* wine last.

THE JURA

This wine region is under the commercial domination of a company founded centuries ago, Henri Maire. There are also many small individual growers. However, despite the efforts of Henri Maire, the Jura wines are not well known in the UK, perhaps because they lack the body for its fickle climate.

APPELLATIONS CONTRÔLÉES
Arbois This appellation produces red, dry white and a *gris* rosé. The reds are made from Pinot Noir and the local grape varieties

Trousseau and Poulsard, either alone or blended. The Trousseau variety lends rich colour and tannin, suitable for a *vin de garde*, while the Poulsard is lightly coloured and makes a rosé even when vinified like a red wine. These rosés derive enough tannin for short-term keeping. The white wines are made from the Savagnin grape (not to be confused with the Sauvignon), the Chardonnay and the Pinot Blanc. The Savagnin can make deeply coloured, sherry-like wines.

The local specialities are *vin de paille* and *vin jaune*, and these are both a must. Neither are appellations. *Vin de paille* is an expensive rarity produced from sugar-rich, sun-dried grapes, dried on *lits de pailles* (straw mats). This is sold only in 62 cl bottles called *pots*. *Vin jaune* is a cask-aged wine exposed, rather like sherry, to air and a *flor* yeast. Having survived this, the *vin jaune* is expensive, complex in flavour and virtually indestructible. It is sold in a squat 62 cl bottle called a *clavelin*. The best *vin jaune* comes from *Château Chalon*.

Under the Arbois AC, *mousseux* wines are also produced.

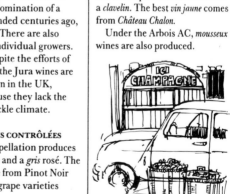

Jura Again, red, dry white and *gris* rosé wines produced from the same grapes as in Arbois. There is also *mousseux*.

Arbois Pupillin These are red, dry white and rosé wines from the commune of Pupillin. They have an added intensity of flavour.

L'Etoile White wine with a little more finesse than straight Arbois. An excellent *mousseux* also exists.

Awaiting the grape harvest

Museums and Châteaux

Champagne houses, particularly the larger ones, are well accustomed to welcoming visitors. Most offer tours and tastings, and direct sales of their wines. Some even have their own museums. A few make a charge for visits that include tastings. Telephone in advance for details.

CANARD DUCHÊNE

In the small village of Ludes-le-Coquet, this modest firm makes outstanding champagne. Visitors are welcomed by a huge 'Visite Des Caves' wall sign, and tastings are offered.
1 Rue Edmond Canard, Ludes, 51500 Rilly-La-Montagne.
Tel (26) 61–10–96.
Open Mon–Fri, 9–11.15am and 2–4pm.

MERCIER

The founder of this Moët-owned firm, Eugène Mercier, went to extraordinary lengths to promote his products. One spectacular scheme was the Mercier cask he commissioned for the Paris Exhibition in 1889. The stupendous, ornate barrel took twenty years to make, could contain 200,000 bottles of champagne – and was hauled from Epernay to Paris by a team of twenty-four white oxen. The largest cask in the world, it now forms a centrepiece of the Mercier cellars tour, which is conducted aboard a miniature train around the company's eleven miles of galleries. There is

An autumnal view of Ober, surrounded by vineyards

a small wine museum, and tastings are offered.
73 Avenue de Champagne, 512000 Epernay.
Tel (26) 51–74–74.
Open Mon–Sat, 9.30am–12 noon and 2–5.30pm; Sun, 9.30am–12.30pm and 2–4.30pm.

MOËT & CHANDON

Largest and most celebrated of the *grandes marques*, Moët's Epernay headquarters are appropriately imposing, complete with magnificent formal gardens and a perfect copy of the Petit Trianon at Versailles built in honour of an important customer – Napoleon. There are guided tours through parts of the seventeen miles of cellars. Attractive museum, and tastings.
18 Avenue de Champagne, 51200 Epernay.
Tel (26) 54–71–11.
Open Mon–Fri, 9.30am–12.30pm, and 2–5.30pm; weekends Apr–Oct.

curious, English/Gothic-style castle built in the 1870s by Louise Pommery – who established the firm as one of the leading *grandes marques*.
5 Place du General Giraud, 51100 Reims.
Tel (26) 05–05–01.
Open Mon–Fri, 9–11am and 2–5pm; weekend tours at 10 and 11am and 2.30, 3.30 and 4.30pm.

TAITTINGER

The beautiful cellars of Taittinger (pronounced Tat-in-jer), deep under the site of the ancient St Nicaise Abbey, which was razed in the French Revolution, are visited by 150,000 people a year. Thirteenth-century monks adapted the original Roman excavations into today's magnificent galleries.
9 Place Saint-Nicaise, 51100 Reims.
Tel (26) 85–45–35.
Open daily, 9am–12noon and 2–6pm.

MUSÉE DU VIN DE CHAMPAGNE

A modest museum in a converted private house, with displays devoted to champagne-making. Highlights include a faithful model of the Abbey at Hautvillers (now owned by Moët) where Dom Pérignon did his pioneering work.
13 Avenue de Champagne, 51200 Epernay.
Tel (26) 51–90–31.
Open daily except Tue 10am–12noon and 2–6pm.

GH MUMM

This image-conscious *maison* has smart new visitor facilities, including film shows devoted to champagne-making. Tours and tastings are available daily.
29–34 Rue de Champs-de-Mars, 51100 Reims.
Tel (26) 40–22–73.
Open Mon–Fri, 9–11am and 2–5pm.

PIPER-HEIDSIECK

A tour aboard an electric train takes visitors through ten miles of cellars – and a century of military history. There was fighting in these galleries in the Franco-Prussian war of 1870, bombardment by the Germans in 1916 and, in the Second World War, a Resistance arsenal was concealed here.
51 Boulevard Henri Vasnier, 51100 Reims.
Tel (26) 85–01–94.
Open Mon–Fri, 9.30–11.30am and 2–5.30pm; weekends Mar 22–Nov 11.

POMMERY

A magnificent stairway of 116 steps leads down to the cool depths first excavated in the chalk by the Romans, whose pits have now been adapted and extended to provide Pommery's eleven miles of cellars. There are some striking bas-relief tableaux carved in the chalk walls. Above, the offices are housed in the

Veuve Clicquot's press house in Verzy

ALSACE

The *Route des Vins* that threads through the vineyards and villages is marked all along the way by billboards that boast of *Caves de Dégustation* – tastings in the cellars. In some of the grander Alsace growers' establishments, this hospitality is extended to tours of the wineries. It is important to telephone for an appointment in advance.

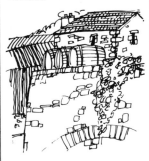

DOPFF AU MOULIN

A family museum – Dopffs have been in the wine business here since 1574 – and the fine cellars are included on a visit to this major firm, picturesquely located on the edge of medieval Riquewihr. In Dopff's Hostellerie Au Moulin the

company's highly rated wines are on sale by the glass, along with a range of authentic Alsacien dishes.
2 Avenue J-Preiss, 68340 Riquewihr.
Tel (89) 47–92–23.
Open Apr 1–Oct 31, daily, 8am (9am weekends)–12noon and 2–6pm.
Hostellerie open all year but closed Tues am and Wed.

HUGEL

More than 3 million bottles of wine slumber in the great cellars beneath the quaintly gabled Riquewihr buildings of Alsace's best-known winemaker. Look out for the immense St Catherine Vat in the cellars. It holds more than 10,000 bottles, and was made in 1715.
3 Rue de la 1ère Armée, 68340 Riquewihr.
Tel (89) 47–92–12.
Open Jul 1–Sep 30, Mon–Thu, 9.30am–12noon and 2–5.30pm; Fri am only.

KUENTZ-BAS

On the Route des Vins a short drive south-west from Colmar, Husseren-Les-Châteaux is home to this firm founded by the Swiss Kuentz family in 1795. Visits take in the cellars and winery and there are tastings – and wines for

sale – in the delightful reception room.
14 Route des Vins, Husseren-Les-Châteaux, 68420 Herrlischeim.
Tel (89) 49–30–24.
Open daily, 9am–6pm.

TRIMBACH

Bernard and Hubert Trimbach, present owners of this renowned firm, are eleventh generation descendants of the founder, who first made wine in Alsace in 1626. Visits and tastings are by appointment only.
68150 Ribeauvillé.
Tel (89) 73–60–30.

MUSÉE DU VIGNOBLE ET DES VINS D'ALSACE

On three floors of the annexe to the local wine association's splendid château, the museum

brims with the picturesque artefacts of the winemaking process, from the cultivation of vines to the pressing (one press on display dates from 1716) and bottling. Glasswork displays trace the craft's history back to the 15th Century.
Château de la Confrérie St-Etienne, Kientzheim, 68240 Kaysersberg. Tel (89) 78–21–36. Open Jul 1–Sep 30, daily, 10am–12noon and 2–6pm.

MUSÉE UNTERLINDEN

Housed in a 13th-century Dominican monastery, this is one of the loveliest museums in France, with a fabulous collection of medieval and Renaissance art–plus a major exhibition devoted to Alsace wine and winemaking. Entry fee is 15FF – and well worth it.
1 Place Unterlinden, 6800 Colmar. Tel (89) 41–89–23. Open daily, 9am–12noon and 2–6pm (closes 5pm and all day Tue Nov 1–Mar 30).

THE JURA

The region's wines are not widely known outside the Jura itself, so a visit to one or more of the *vignerons* offers an opportunity to discover some new and distinctive styles and flavours. It is wise to telephone in advance.

JEAN BOURDY

Founded in 1781, Caves Jean Bourdy have an unpretentious *maison* in the village of Arlay. Visitors are offered tastings from the excellent range of Bourdy wines, which include a rare and very fine *vin de paille*.
Arlay 39140 Bletterans. Tel (84) 85–03–70. Open Mon–Sat, 9am–12noon and 2–7pm.

CHÂTEAU D'ARLAY

This extensive estate incorporates the romantically gaunt ruins of a huge fortress that was home to the local aristocracy until its destruction by Louis XI in the 1470s, in the process of transferring power from provincial nobles back to the throne. Here, too, is the majestic 18th-century château that is now home to today's aristocratic master of Arlay, Comte Renaud de Laguiche. Marvellous to visit, and tastings of the wines are offered.
Arlay 39140 Bletterans. Tel (84) 85–04–22. Open Jul 1–Aug 31 daily; Sep 1–Jun 30 Mon–Fri, 9am–12noon and 2–6pm; weekends by appointment only.

CHÂTEAU DE L'ETOILE

A large house rather than a château *per se*, presiding over the small *appellation L'Etoile controlée* under which a mere 200,000 litres of wine are made annually. Tastings offered.
L'Etoile, 39570 Lons-Le-Saunier. Tel (84) 47–33–07. Open Mon–Sat, 8am–12noon and 3–5pm.

HENRI MAIRE

The major winemaker of the region, this firm takes its public relations seriously. The large Henri Maire centre in Arbois offers tastings and film shows (not entirely devoted to Maire wines, as one film depicts the life of Arbois' most famous son, Louis Pasteur) and a shop. There are tours of the cellars and, by bus, of the vineyards.
Les Deux Tonneaux, Rue de l'Hôtel de Ville, 39600 Arbois. Tel. (84) 66–12–34. Open daily 9am–7.30pm.

MUSÉE DE LA VIGNE ET DU VIN

The cellars below the town hall, formerly a convent dating from the 14th Century, have displays of local winemaking materials and techniques. Louis Pasteur's work in viniculture is brought arrestingly to life in a special exhibition.
Hôtel de Ville, 39600 Arbois. Tel (84) 66–07–45. Open daily Jul 1–Aug 31 and weekends only in Jun, 3–7pm, and on demand out of season by telephoning M. Jouvenot (84) 66–04–19.

The town of Arbois seen from its vineyards

Gastronomic Specialities

Munster cheeses in a Kaysersberg fromagerie

CHAMPAGNE & THE AUBE

AU CHAMPAGNE on a menu signifies a dish cooked with the wine of the region. But this is likely to be with the still red or white *Coteaux Champenois* wines rather than the costly sparkling variety. The bubbles, of course, disappear immediately champagne is heated.

BISCUITS DE REIMS are the small, oblong macaroon biscuits traditionally offered with a glass of apéritif champagne.

ANDOUILLETTES are the rich and exotic sausages of northern France (made largely from tripe and intestines of calf or pig) and come in a famous variation from Troyes in the Aube.
ANDOUILLETTES DE MOUTON. These are strongly flavoured, peppery, and should be slightly moist. Made entirely from sheep.

BROCHET The pike is among several local river fish at the heart of regional speciality dishes. The flesh of the pike is commonly pounded into a fibrous paste and made into fish balls or sausage shapes, sometimes with potato included, served with a rich sauce. Look out for delicious *cervelat de brochet*, and *pain à la reine* – pike mousse.

Among Champagne cheeses worth discovering are CAPRICE DES DIEUX, a soft, full-fat, cow's-milk variety in the shape of a small, oval loaf, and MAROILLES, a square cow's-milk slab with a sheeny red-brown rind and pungently delicious flavour. Cendre de Champagne – so known after its coating with CENDRES (ashes) – is a flat disc, again cow's milk, with a mild smell but excellent, slightly nutty, flavour; at its best in summer. Cylindrical, cow's milk CHAOURCE is delicate in flavour with a fine aroma, reminiscent of mushrooms; soft but firm, and very good.

PAIN D'ÉPICE, a spicy-sweet cake, and GOUGÉRE DE L'AUBE, a light cheese bread, are local specialities to try from the region's pâtisseries.

PÂTÉ EN CROÛTE CHAMPENOIS. The Champagne version of the hot pâté in pastry that is popular all over France includes chunks of goose meat. In Reims, pigeon *pâté en croûte* is a speciality.

POTÉE CHAMPENOISE is midway between a soup and a stew – a warming *compote* of pork and ham with lots of vegetables, among which potatoes figure largely. Chicken and sausages are sometimes included. A traditional dish at the time of harvest – when the weather may well be turning chilly.

ALSACE

A L'ALSACIENNE is used to describe dishes in which *choucroute* (the very superior sauerkraut of the region) or other preparations of cabbage are included.

BAECKAOFFA A classic Alsace stew of beef, lamb and pork marinated first in wine, then casseroled in layers interspersed with sliced potatoes and onions. The name means 'baker's oven'.

Strasbourg, regional capital of Alsace, also has a reputation as the sausage capital of France. Throughout the region, **SAUCISSES** of every variety certainly make Alsace *charcuteries* a special attraction. **SAUCISSE DE STRASBOURG**, made of smoked pork and beef, resembles the British sausage in shape and size, and has a slightly smoky flavour, spiced with caraway seeds.

CHOUCROUTE is very much the dish of the region. Alsace cabbage – in this case a large, white variety called *chou quintal* – makes for perfect pickling, and making *choucroute* is a substantial local industry, complete with its own annual festival in Colmar. *Choucroute Alsacienne* is a filling dish of *choucroute, saucisses de Strasbourg*, pork, bacon, juniper berries, garlic and potatoes – all cooked in Riesling wine.

TRUITE AU BLEU River fish supply some fine local specialities. Trout *au bleu* is so known from the colour the fish turn (though they must be very

freshly caught to oblige) when simmered for six minutes in *court bouillon* – Riesling wine with a little vinegar, and flavoured with onion and carrot.

MUNSTER Alsace's delicious soft cheese, at its best straight from the farms in the Vosges mountains, is strong and tangy – and when very young (which is how the Alsaciens like it) can be eaten with a spoon! Marvellous with a glass of Gewürztraminer.

KOUGELHOPF The light, brioche-style, cake of Alsace is made in the shape of a narrow-brimmed hat with a hole in the centre. It is flavoured and decorated with sultanas and almonds.

THE JURA

POULET AUX MORILLES This classic dish encapsulates the flavours of the Jura – its excellent poultry, the intense pungency of its truffle-like wild mushrooms, *morilles* (see later entry), and a cream sauce prepared with the dry, sherry-like wine of the region, *vin jaune*.

Jura. They are available fresh only in late April and May (but must be cooked; they are poisonous raw) and otherwise can be bought dried.

COMTÉ The well-known cheese of France-Comté, immediately to the south of the Jura, is a mild, slightly salty, hard cheese in the Gruyère style, with pea-sized holes. The terms *au comté* and *comtoise* apply to the many dishes made with this excellent cheese.

CROUSTADE JURASSIENNE Comté cheese and bacon are the main ingredients for this delicious fried toast snack flavoured with onions and nutmeg.

Taking a break at Colmar market

JÉSUS DE MORTEAU This unusually named sausage is made from shoulder of pork, traditionally smoked over juniper wood.

MORILLES These pointed fungi with their brown, pitted caps, are the most prized – and by far the most expensive – of several wild mushroom varieties found in the

PETS DE NONNE These choux-pastry fritters, made from dough flavoured with lemon or orange and deep fried, are traditionally served with a hot jam sauce. The name derives from a venerable convent at Baume-les-Dames in France-Comté which had a great culinary reputation. *Pets de nonne* translates, unavoidably, into 'nun's farts'.

Hotels and Restaurants

AUBERGE DU RELAIS

Small and friendly restaurant in the happily named village of Dizy. Good value. Closed Mon evening and all Tue.
Dizy, 51200 Epernay.
Tel (26) 55–25–11.

AUX ARMES DE CHAMPAGNE

At L'Epine, eight kilometres west of Chalons-sur-Marne, this very comfortable hotel has 40 rooms, reasonable prices and an exceptional, Michelin-starred restaurant. Specialities include *magret* (duck breast) cooked in a truffle and champagne-vinegar sauce.
L'Epine, 51460 Courtisois.
Tel (26) 66–96–79.

LES BERCEAUX

Hotel-restaurant with a particular welcome for British guests, as owner and chef Luc Maillard's wife – and partner – Jill, is English. Rooms are comfortable, and fish the speciality of the relaxed dining room. Reasonable prices. Restaurant closed Sun evening.
13 Rue des Berceaux, 51200 Epernay.
Tel (26) 55–28–84.

LA BRIQUETERIE

Smart country hotel with grand gardens and a restaurant serving serious food. Fresh *foie gras* is a speciality. Pricey.
Route de Sézanne, Vinay, 51200 Epernay.
Tel (26) 51–47–12.

LE CHARDONNAY

Justifiably popular restaurant with an excellent menu (the set menus are particularly good value) and a vast range of champagnes at tempting prices. Elegant surroundings but a bustling, friendly atmosphere. Closed Sat lunch and Sun all day.
184 Avenue Epernay, 51100 Reims.
Tel (26) 06–08–60.

LES CRAYÈRES

So known because it is built above the *crayères* (chalk pits) that are now the cellars of Reims, this very grand hotel-restaurant is owned by Pommery, whose elaborate gothic buildings it overlooks across an elegant park. Food and wine are magnificent (three stars in *Michelin*) and prices appropriately elevated. Restaurant closed all Mon, and Tue lunch.
64 Boulevard Vasnier, 51100 Reims.
Tel. (26) 82–80–80.

ROYAL CHAMPAGNE

Stylish hotel-restaurant well located on a hillside and commanding fine views over the vineyards of the Marne Valley. Popular with members of the Champagne trade, it is busy and friendly, though not inexpensive. Fish dishes outstanding.
Champillon Bellvue, 51160 Ay.
Tel (26) 51–11–51.

The isolated church of Chavot, near Moussy

Autumn in the vineyards at Epernay

LE VIGNERON

Quirky restaurant in the rustic style, serving traditional Champagne cuisine prepared with consummate skill by the extravagantly moustached owner-chef, Hervé Liegent.
Place Jamot, 51100 Reims.
Tel (26) 47–00–71.

ALSACE

AUBERG DE L'ILL

Rated by the guides – *Michelin* gives it the ultimate accolade of three stars – as probably the best restaurant in Alsace, this riverside inn offers extraordinary standards of cooking and wine. Prices are relatively reasonable. Closed Mon (except for lunch in summer) and Tue.
Rue de Collonges, Illhaeusern, 68150 Ribeauvillé.
Tel (89) 71–83–23.

AUBERGE DU PÈRE FLORANC

Inn with comfortable rooms, and a highly rated restaurant. Warm, friendly atmosphere in which to enjoy such specialities as *tourte de caille* (quail tart) and *quatre foies gras de l'auberge*. Fair prices. Closed Sun evening and Mon all day.

9 Rue Herzog, Wettolsheim, 68000 Colmar.
Tel. (89) 41–39–14.

CAVEAU D'EGUISHEIM

Cellar restaurant in the highly picturesque village of Eguisheim. Small, intimate and with a very good, inexpensive menu. *Choucroute* dishes a speciality. Closed Wed evening and Thu all day.
3 Place du Château St-Leon, Eguisheim, 68420 Herrlisheim.
Tel. (89) 41–08–89.

CHAMBARD

A modern hotel-restaurant built in the traditional Alsace style with steep gables and angular turrets, this strange-looking place offers excellent cooking at sensible prices. *La pièce de boeuf au*

pinot noir et à la moelle (beef fillet in red wine and rich stock) and *navarin de homard aux cepes* (lobster stew with local mushrooms) are among the superb specialities. Closed Sun evening and all day Mon.
13 Rue de Genérale de Gaulle, 68240 Kaysersberg.
Tel (89) 47–10–17.

CHATEAU D'ISENBOURG

A luxurious Relais du Chateau hotel beautifully situated up in the foothills of the Vosges, with fine views of the vineyards below. As usual with this standard of hotel, there is a swimming pool and tennis court – and commensurate prices. But the restaurant, though highly rated, is good value.
Rouffac, 68250 Haut-Rhin.
Tel (89) 49–63–53.

LE CLOSE ST VINCENT

This very attractive inn among the vines has panoramic views from its hillside vantage point. Rooms – there are only 11 – are quiet and stylish. The restaurant is small and welcoming. Good food but not cheap. Restaurant closed Tue and Wed.
Route de Bergheim, Ribeauvillé, 68150 Haut-Rhin.
Tel (89) 73–67–65.

L'ECURIE

Restaurant in a converted stable in the delightfully picturesque village of Riquewihr. Popular with tourists, it offers a simple menu and fair value. Closed Thu.
Riquewihr 68430.
Tel (89) 47–92–48.

HOTEL ARNOLD

Comfortable hotel in the Hostellerie du Vignoble association – very picturesque, especially in spring and summer when the whole of the gabled front positively blazes with geranium blooms. Good restaurant serving regional specialities. Very fair value.
98 Route de Vin, 67140 Ittersmiller (Bas-Rhin).
Tel (88) 85–50–58.

MAISON DES TÊTES

In a sublime 17th-Century house in classical Alsace style, this amiable restaurant offers authentic Alsacien cuisine at good prices. Wonderful terrines and pâtés, and *choucroute* galore. Closed Sun evening and Mon all day.
19 Rue des Têtes, 68000 Colmar.
Tel (89) 24–43–43.

Looking east towards the Rhine and the Black Forest

Arbois in the Jura

HOSTELLERIE MONTS DE VAUX

Very comfortable hotel-restaurant with stylish rooms. Fairly expensive but well located for exploring the region. Restaurant closed Tue all day and Wed lunch.
Monts de Vaux, 39800 Poligny. Tel (84) 37–12–50.

MOULIN DE LA MÈRE MICHELLE

Sheltered by the rocky cliffs, this modest *auberge* stands by the source of the Cuisance river, where a grand watermill once worked. The present building dates from 1830. Ten rooms, and a small restaurant offering traditional Jura fare – including delicious *Poulardo de Bresse aux morilles et vin jaune*. Closed from Nov 15 to Mar 15.
Les Planches, 39600 Arbois. Tel (84) 66–08–17.

RELAIS D'ALSACE

Good food and fair prices prevail in this simple but attractive restaurant in Lons-Le-Saunier, just south of the L'Etoile district. Closed Sun evening and Mon all day.
74 Route Besançon, Lons-Le-Saunier, 39000 Jura. Tel (84). 47–24–70.

REVERMONT HOTEL

A quiet and rather unprepossessing hotel with good modern facilities – swimming and tennis included – and peaceful gardens. Simple restaurant. Inexpensive. Closed Jan and Feb. Restaurant closed Sun evening and Mon in winter.
Passenans, 39230 Sellières. Tel (84) 44–61–02.

THE JURA

BELLE-VUE

Lakeside restaurant with high standards of cooking and high prices by the standards of the Jura. There are a few bedrooms. Closed Sun evening and Mon all day.
25160 Malbuisson. Tel (81) 69–30–89.

DE PARIS

Restaurant with rooms in a medieval building – and the only rated eating place in Arbois. Regional specialities include *gigot de poularde au vin jaune et aux morilles* (chicken in wild mushroom and wine sauce). Not cheap. Closed Mon evening and Tue all day outside school holidays.
Rue de l'Hôtel de Ville, 39600 Arbois. Tel (84) 66–05–67.

Calendar of Events

MARCH

1st week – Wine competition at the Porte de Versailles in Paris

2nd Sunday – Presentation of new wines in Eguisheim (Haut-Rhin)

APRIL/MAY

Porte de Versailles in Paris – Wine competition at the Porte de Versailles

MAY

1st – Wine fair in Molsheim (Bas-Rhin)

Ascension – Wine fair in Guebwiller (Haut-Rhin)

JUNE

3rd weekend – Petit Vin Blanc Festival in Nogent-sur-Marne (Marne) – alternate years, next 1989

11th – Kugelhopf (cake) fair in Ribeauvillé (Bas-Rhin)

Saturday nearest 24th – Festival of St John in Cumières (Marne)

Saturday nearest 24th – Festival of St John in Epernay (Marne)

Saturday nearest 24th – Festival of St John in Hautvillers (Marne)

Saturday nearest 24th – Festival of St John in Rheims (Marne)

JULY

Middle of the month – Wine Fair in Barr (Bas-Rhin)

3rd weekend – Fair in Ribeauvillé (Haut-Rhin)

3rd weekend – Riesling festival in Riquewihr (Haut-Rhin)

Saturday after 14th – Fêtes des Guinguettes d'Europe in Husseren-les-Châteaux (Haut-Rhin)

3rd Sunday – Wine festival in Arbois (Jura)

End of the month – Wine festival in Wettolsheim (Haut-Rhin)

Last weekend – Wine festival in Mittelbergheim (Bas-Rhin)

AUGUST

1st Sunday – Fair of the almond trees in Mittelwihr (Haut-Rhin)

Landscape near Passenans

1st weekend – Alsace wine festival in Bennwihr (Haut-Rhin)

1st weekend – Wine festival, Au Pays du Brans, in Turkheim (Haut-Rhin)

1st fortnight – Regional fair of Alsace wines in Colmar (Haut-Rhin)

1st fortnight – Wine festival in Dambach-la-Ville (Bas-Rhin)

Middle of the month – Wine mini fair in Obernai (Bas-Rhin)

3rd weekend – Festival of arts and crafts of Riesling wines in Scherwiller (Bas-Rhin)

Last Sunday – Vintage festival in Eguisheim (Haut-Rhin)

Last Sunday – Champagne festival of the Aube vineyards in the Aube district once every three years, next 1990

SEPTEMBER

1st Sunday – Fête des ménétriers in Ribeauvillé (Haut-Rhin)

1st Sunday – Fêtes de Biou wine festival in Arbois (Jura)

Beginning of the month – Wine festival in Wolxheim (Bas-Rhin)

13th/14th – Val de St Grégoire festival in Zimmerbach (Haut-Rhin)

2nd Sunday – Festival of St Vincent in Ambonnay (Marne)

2nd Sunday – Champagne wine fair in Bar-sur-Aube (Aube)

3rd week – Harvest festival in Bagneux (Seine-et-Marne)

3rd week – Festival and wine fair in Charly-sur-Marne (Aisne)

Last weekend – Harvest festival in Seltz (Bas-Rhin)

Last weekend – Harvest festival in Valff (Bas-Rhin)

FIRST WEEKS OF OCTOBER

Harvest festivals in various villages of Alsace: Barr, Hunawihr, Itterswiller, Katzenthal, Niedermorschwihr, Obernai, Rosheim

OCTOBER

1st Saturday – Harvest festival in Paris/Montmârtre

1st weekend – Harvest festival in Barr (Bas-Rhin)

1st Sunday – Harvest festival in Suresnes (Seine-et Marne)

1st fortnight – Harvest festival in Hunawihr (Haut-Rhin)

1st fortnight – Harvest festival in Katzenthal (Haut-Rhin)

2nd weekend – Grand Festival of the grape in Molsheim (Bas-Rhin)

3rd weekend – Harvest festival in Marlenheim (Bas-Rhin)

3rd weekend – Harvest festival in Obernai (Bas-Rhin)

3rd week – Wine competition at the Porte de Versailles in Paris

The vineyards of Châteaux Chalon

Index